JACQUES BAINVILLE

TWO HISTORIES
FACE TO FACE

FRANCE V/S GERMANY

WITH A NEW FOREWORD BY THE AUTHOR

TRANSLATED BY PAUL LEFAIVRE

PARIS
NOUVELLE LIBRAIRIE NATIONALE
3, Place du Panthéon, 3

MCMXIX

TWO HISTORIES
FACE TO FACE

BY THE SAME AUTHOR

NOUVELLE LIBRAIRIE NATIONALE

Louis II de Bavière.
Bismarck et la France.
Le Coup d'Agadir et la guerre d'Orient.
Histoire de deux peuples.
Comment est née la révolution russe.
Histoire de trois générations.

A. FAYARD & Cie

La Guerre et l'Italie.

SOCIÉTÉ LITTÉRAIRE DE FRANCE

Petit musée germanique.

HODDER & STOUGHTON, LONDON

Italy and the war.

JACQUES BAINVILLE

TWO HISTORIES FACE TO FACE

FRANCE VERSUS GERMANY

With a new foreword by the author

TRANSLATED
BY
PAUL LEFAIVRE

PARIS
NOUVELLE LIBRAIRIE NATIONALE
3, PLACE DU PANTHÉON, 3

MCMXIX

CONTENTS

FOREWORD

When, on the 4th of August 1914, Germany declared war on France, who was living peaceably, without even dreaming of the possibility of retaking her lost provinces, it was the twentieth time at least, in the course of her history, that the Germans had crossed their rivers in a rush towards the West. Since nearly a thousand years the French nation exists. Since nearly a thousand years, too, she endures the undesirable neighbourhood of the Germanic peoples, always covetous of alien property, as described even by a great historian of antiquity.

France has, therefore, the perilous honor of being the vanguard of the western world against German onslaughts and for many centuries, her principal task has been to protect herself from the assaults of that everlasting foe.

Of course, just as the other European nations, France has, in the course of her history, fought more or less against everybody. She has had a bone to pick now with the British, now with the Italians, with the Spaniards, with the Russians. But these wars had not left inexpiable records. They had been followed by long periods of friendship, of alliances, and of mutual confidence. This is a matter of the past. France is now in security having only friends on all her boundaries, save those to the East, which she must still defend, even as for a thousand years, against a hostile people whose main reason of hatred for her lies doubtless in the fact that it is France who always barred them the way, in their attempts at universal conquest. It is the Germans who forged for us the hateul appellation of " hereditary foes " (Erbfeind), showing clearly that, from generation to generation, their hearts remain the same.

Yet the French nation is so sociable that, in the course of centuries, she has succeeded several times in living on good terms, if not

with all Germans, at least with part of them.
At the brightest periods of French diplomacy,
our great statesmen achieved that masterpiece.
It is true that it was after beating Germany,
and after tearing from her that political and
military might of which she has never been able
to make other than a fatal use for mankind.

The great French quality is good sense.
Each time France neglected to make use of it,
as she did too often in the course of the XIXth
century, the penalty came prompt and severe.
Under the influence of the liberal and humanitarian ideas then so popular everywhere, she did
not object to the creation of a great Germany.
By a generous adhesion to the principle of nationalities, she went further, favoring ingenuously German unification, in the belief that,
once moulded in a single nation, as were the
French themselves, the Germans would prove to
be harmless neighbours and, even, reliable
friends. It is for this very illusion, shared also
by England and by the United States, that we
are paying so heavily to-day: It would have
been undoubtedly much wiser to sift carefully
these same liberal and humanitarian ideas which

were to be turned against us by the Germans, through some foreseeing policy adhering to the precepts of good sense, and which the experience of our ancient diplomatic system had-proved so beneficial to our national evolution. We should foresee that, some day, Germany will handle the ideas of democracy and of the Society of Nations, just as she did that of the principles of nationalities fifty years ago.

It is not enough to be victorious. It is necessary to make the effects of victory lasting. This juxtaposed history of France and Germany, in the course of their secular conflicts, shows under what conditions the Allies can reap the full fruit of their sacrifices and of their efforts.

In order that there may be no German peril, Germany must be politically weakened and divided. Disunited, the Germans become peaceful. They even contribute their share towards universal civilization. They develop whatever qualities they possess. Never were they so happy as during the two centuries when they were a mosaic of little States and never had they so many poets and artists who did honor to their country. But, as soon as they were united, as soon as they formed one great and single nation, the evil in them predominated. They dream of nothing else but abuse of their strength. Therefore no more security for their neighbours, and all has to be done over again.

That is precisely where we are to-day. Three quarters of mankind have been forced to join against the Germans because they had not understood, in 1870, what the defeat of France and the formation of a great and united Germany would mean. This book, in summing up the experiences which, during a thousand years, it has been France's sad privilege to suffer, intends to show the solutions which may be chosen and the mistakes which may be avoided.

Since it was written, many events of great import have occurred. In the first place, the United States have come into the war, bringing their mighty help to France, as France, in the XVIIIth century had come to the rescue of the American colonies fighting for their independence. A hundred and fifty years later, the community of feeling and of interest became fully identified, which is another proof of one of the main ideas developed in this book : that through the chain of the ages, the interest and sympathies of the two peoples are the same.

The other event is the wreck of Russia. About the time that the United States entered the war, Russia became a Republic. This advent of democracy in what was once the huge and powerful Russian Empire, was in no way auspicious for the cause of the Allies. The war would have ended long ago, with our victory, had the countless armies of the Tsar held together. Russian democracy, on the contrary, signed at Brest-Litovsk a shameful capitulation with the Imperial staffs : A valuable lesson teaching us once again the folly of ready made phrases and of too absolute formulæ. We know what France paid for her democratic intoxication. We now see the same folly playing havoc in Russia at the Allies expense.

As the sun of victory, which the avenging banners of the Entente carry in their folds, is about to rise, it seems to us that the moment has come to offer to our Anglo-Saxon allies a synoptic survey of the century-old duel between France and Germany, and whose last phases are so momentous for us all.

You, millions of Americans and British, who tread our soil, breathe our air, study our language, work and fight with us, elbow to elbow, and mingle your blood with ours, are you not entitled to receive the freedom of our country for generations to come? If, as it is said, the future is often but the recurring past, you will perhaps better understand, after turning over these pages, the circumstances of the future which is to be yours, in the light of the past that is ours. We shall not have paid too high a price for our common victory if you realize the permanent foundations on which must rest our common liberation from the clutch of the German hydra : that this peace must be historically, geographically and economically a strictly French peace, if you would have it be your own peace as well.

JACQUES BAINVILLE.

1918.

TWO
HISTORIES FACE TO FACE
FRANCE VERSUS GERMANY

CHAPTER I

THE HEREDITARY MONARCHY OF THE CAPETIANS
AND GERMAN ANARCHY

As soon as the perseverance of several generations of Capets[1] had resulted in endowing France with a personality, the problem of the Eastern boundary loomed in sight. The Kingdom having expanded found itself suddenly striking against a hostile people, Germany,

1. Third race of the kings of France, beginning with Hugues Capet. Direct Capetians from Hughes Capet to Charles IV le Bel (987-1328) ; Capetians Valois, from Philippe VI to Henri III (1328-1589) ; Capetians Bourbons from Henri IV to Louis-Philippe (1589-1848).

standing as a sentinel watching the Rhine, and it was precisely towards the Rhine itself that France spread out, that its shape might complete and perfect itself, and thus become as it were classical and satisfying to mind and reason.

A true instinct of leadership impelled the dukes of France, heirs of the Gallo-Roman traditions, to rebuild the Gaul of Cæsar. And it was already evident that, so far as Germany was concerned, the struggle would be hard and long... So hard, so long that even in the xx[th] century, far from being finished, it was to break out again under the most inhuman, the most terrific conditions the world has ever known, since the invasions of the barbarian hordes. On five sides of the hexagon the successors of Hugues Capet[1] had traced France's form and limits... They disappeared before their task was achieved. And the work of so many generations has been damaged, imperiled just on that North-Eastern boundary, so long the aim of the French nation's effort.

1. 946-996. — Proclaimed King of France, 987.

The English menace was evident at several periods of our history but for France it was not the most serious. More than once, the British have had interests in common with us. But if they start a conflict, if they cross the Channel, they can be hurled into the sea, thrown out from the kingdom, be begged to keep within their island limits. But the German ?

He lives with us, side by side, in the closest intimacy; he communicates through our valleys and our rivers. Push the German mass back at one point, thanks to its plasticity, it will reappear on another, and France will be in danger of invasion so long as she has not these limits which, from the beginning, were called natural, because they are our essential boundaries. France will not be safe so long as the geographical neighbourhood of Germany oppresses her and German armies are but at a few days' march from Paris, France, even in time of peace, is menaced by that prolific and migratory people always ready to settle in another's nest. Germany, in her turn, considers it a vital blow whenever she is driven beyond the Rhine, when she gives over, to the influence of the French language and civilisation, the Germanic colonies fixed on the former domain of Imperial Gaul. So it is that through the past centuries Lothair's[1] Kingdom has been disputed ground. All the solutions that have been tried, all the political combinations resorted to, have proved powerless to settle the old contest. The Kingdom of Belgium, the Grand Duchy of Luxemburg, Imperial domains, these expedients which succeeded to the ancient cities so pertinently called " frontier cities of the barrier," and which to-day mark our boundaries, were, at the beginning, simple matters of arbitrage. Frontier States, were enabled to grow into nations in all the force of the term, as Belgium has shown so magnificently. But the frontiers of the East and North-East remain battlefields which no one has ever succeeded in neutralizing in any definite manner.

From Bouvines[2] to Sedan and La Marne,

1. Lothaire II, great-grand-son of Charlemagne. He was king of Lorraine (869).

2. Near Lille, where Philippe Auguste, with the support of French militias, defeated Emperor Othon IV (1214).

twenty times have the French and the German peoples risen face to face. The wars, the combats were but the explosion of perpetual rivalry. During the truces, sometimes of long duration, political and diplomatic action continued the efforts of the armies at rest, and tended, through the advantages gained by one or other to reduce the rival to impotence. France, thanks to special political conditions, was the nation who most often got the upper hand.

Parsimonious of French blood, the hereditary guardians of our security justly made use of all and any circumstances to disarm the German giant, to divide him against himself, to distract his attention. These circumstances, in case of need, could always be provoked. The Kingdom of Germany had, at the start, a large advance over the Kingdom of France. The German State had even grown to adult years before a French State existed. It was necessary to take advantage of all the weak spots in the huge cuirass, to exercise a close watch over Germany's troubles, quarrels and embarrassments. It was necessary to intervene actively in the interior policy of Germany. Thus was written the history of an endless struggle, extending over a series of centuries, but in which, wars of extermination not being conceivable between such numerous populations, calculation and skill were bound to prevail. Of the two nations, that one endowed with the best brain would win the game.

The eminently practical genius of the Capetian kings, especially clever in taking advantage of events, quick to learn the lessons of experience, had not been mistaken concerning the way to deal with the German problem. The proof that they were right is found in the results obtained, marvelous results if one compares the humble dukedom of France to the powerful realm of Germany, the remainder of the Carolingian [1] Empire.

That the French Monarchy had committed some errors in the application of its

1. Carolingians, or Carlovingians; second dynasty of the kings of France, drawing its name from Charlemagne (751-987).

policy, — that it was not infallible, nobody
will doubt. What strikes the mind is that
she never persisted in any mistake and,
especially, that she never varied regarding
the principles nor forgot the aims in view.
Unhandy turns in the wheel were repaired in
good time, the direction changed at the first
sign that the wrong way had been taken.
There were too moments in the diplomatic
history of the ancient regime, where awk-
ward errors nearly spoiled everything :
under Louis XIII, at the battle of the White
Mountain[1], and under Louis XV, in the
first Seven Years'War[2]. But nothing was
lost then, because the principles of leadership, even if misunderstood, had never been
disregarded.

He was, indeed, but a small lord, that
French king of the first Capetian generations,
facing the powerful Roman Emperor of the

1. Thirty Years'war first period.   Known as the Palatinate
period; Frederick, elector of the Palatinate elected King of
Bohemia, was vanquished at the battle of the White Mountain (1620) and despoiled of his States.
2. War of the Succession of Austria (1741-1748).

Germanic nation, heir to Charlemagne, successor of the Cæsars, " the other half of God ; " and who claimed supremacy over all the Christian world. There was a century when this claim nearly became reality, when the common belief was that the Holy Empire would rule the whole of Christendom. Till then, the Imperial diadem had been bestowed by election. Barbarossa and his successors who represented the German idea in the xii[th] and xiii[th] centuries, as the Hohenzollerns represent it nowadays, had undertaken nothing less than to unite all the German countries in order to extend later on their power over the whole of Europe. The first step in this plan was to consolidate the Imperial authority. Deprived of the benefit of heredity, usufructuaries of an elective crown which, at each new reign, put everything again in question, the Hohenstaufens[1] had no strong belief in the realization of their ambitious aims. The direct transmission of the crown through inheritance appeared to them

1. Illustrious Imperial family, from Würtemberg (1138-1250).

as the essential condition of political power.

However, the Capetian monarchy, whose modest beginnings had aroused nobody's jealousy nor attention, had already succeeded in getting rid of the elective system. As early as the 5th generation, the successors of Hugues Capet obtained that advantage. Therefore, feeling themselves firm in the saddle, they turned their eyes towards Lorraine, towards Flanders, and all those other Imperial states which they rightly considered as French countries. At the same time, a sure instinct warned the Capetians that, if the Kings of Germany should become independent like themselves, if a Hohenstaufen should obtain that privilege of hereditary right which was at the bottom of their own strength, young France would be threatened by a most serious danger, the future of the dynasty founded by Hugues Capet would be imperiled, and perhaps for ever.

This was a primary interest which was to be damaged in the person of the French kings, by the ambitions of the Hohenstaufens. Assisted by a force no longer to be disregarded, supported by a nation every day more conscious of its migth, the Capetians were already strong enough to oppose serious difficulties to the plots of their German rivals. But, there was elsewhere in Europe, another power which felt itself also threatened by the ambitions of the heirs of Charlemagne : the Pope. who would hardly admit that the Emperor, his partner in the Government of the world, should free himself from the common pact. The first '' half of God '' feared that the second one might reduce it to slavery and so destroy the spiritual and temporal balance. The Imperial power was submitted to the double servitude of the election and of the consecration. The Church understood that, once freed from the first, the Emperor would try to avoid the other. Moreover, experience had taught her to fear, for her own independence, that overwhelming power accrue to the Holy German Empire. Thus she realized that the benefit of heredity would inevitably endow it with a tremendous increase of strength.

Therefore, just as the young French kingdom had done, the Holy See made her's the principle that it was a vital necessity to check the ambitions of the Hohenstaufens. In Paris as in Rome, the " statu quo " in Germany was chosen as the best solution prudence could suggest to prevent the great political change dreamed of by the Emperor. A junction was naturally bound to occur, an alliance was certain to knot itself between these two identical interests. Hence a community of views was born which was to last through the centuries, in spite of the accidents, the passions, the misunderstandings and even the circumstances, which, from time to time, separated Rome from France, without ever entirely breaking a tie formed by the very nature of things and by the necessities of policy.

Behind that effort of the Hohenstaufens to acquire hereditary rule, there was the aim to complete, after all, the German Kingdom. It was the question of German unity which was laid before Europe of the Middle Ages, as it would be before Europe of the Renaissance and before Europe of to-day.

It was the peril of the Teutonic power threatening to become unbearable which already was frightening all political minds. Therefore, outside opposition gave rise to the principle of maintaining and developing the anarchy and divisions in Germany. From that moment began the era of foreign interventions, of diplomatic combinations, in order to keep " the Germanies " in the condition of particularism to which they had been brought by the feudal parcelling, but a condition still further aggravated by the system of an elective monarchy, so that in the Middle Ages already, before the great interregnum, Germany responded to the definition given of her, later on, by Frederick the 2nd : " A noble Republic of Princes. "

For, if Germany, like Italy, remained so long divided, it was not because a mysterious fate had so willed it. Neither can it be ascribed to the configuration of the soil, or to the character of the people. That kind of predestination is simply a matter of fancy. Germany and Italy have proved, in the last 4o years, that unity was in their nature just as well as particularism. Italy's limits are as distinct as those of Germany are indistinct. Both, still, have experienced by turns the system of a single government and that of many princes. To M. Ernest Lavisse we owe the remark that : " In the xth century, among all the countries which had composed Charlemagne's inheritance, Germany seemed the one nearest to unity. " This unity, almost a fact, was unmade. A little later, it was decidedly missed, and its opportunities did not reappear until modern times. What directed this destiny? Again, M. Lavisse points out : " Germany, at the time of her decadence, was unable to take advantage of that continuity in monarchic action by which other countries were built up as States which later on became nations. "

While in France the royal function reached the climax of its power, the German monarchy met with all kinds of difficulties and obstacles. We have noted the enmities which arose against it from the outside. At home, the antagonists she had to face were in no way less redoutable. The institution of heredity had been easily realized by Hugues Capet's dynasty which, in those days, awakened nobody's suspicion and was much weaker than many of the great feudal lords. But the Hohenstaufen family, at the time it tried to free itself from the electors and their control, could not flatter itself that it was unnoticed. Already Germany had become a formidable figure. In Europe, there was a general feeling that she aimed at a world supremacy, and that within her boundaries, she dreamed of a despotic form of government. Her splendour was at the same time her weakness. The same thing happened later on to the Habsburgs[1] with Charles V[th] and his successors, while the modest Marquesses of Brandeburg awakened distrust but only among a few rare minds gifted with prevision.

One understands now why any attempt of the Emperor to emancipate his crown from the elective system united against him the various elements which feared the rising of a strong power in Germany.

1. Rodolf I., of Habsburg, founder of the Austrian Monarchy, in 1273.

At home the simple prospect of the State being represented by a monarchy met, — as was always the case in Germany, in France, everywhere, — opposition on the part of interests which, then as now, had the sweet habit of thriving at the expense of the commonwealth, opposed to the public welfare and to the conditions of that welfare which rests upon the independence of the State. All sorts of Princes, Dukes, burgraves, Rhin graves, all that dust of the Teutonic dynasts of the Middle Ages, feared, and hated the dynasty which would at once restrain the powers of the small Sovereigns. Likewise, the ecclesiastic Lords, the mercantile oligarchies, the Hanseatic League, the free cities, the peasant democracies (whose remnants are the Swiss cantons), the pieces, infinitely diverse, in a word, of the German mosaic, wanted to preserve their very fruitful liberty. According to a very human concept, they thought that, so long as the power remains elective, there is some profit to be drawn from each election. Either by according universal suffrage, or by the most re-

stricted to be imagined, an election means
and has always meant a business, a bargain, a
job. Its character of barter appears the more
commercial the smaller the number of electors
and the more weight carried by the individual ticket. Selling their votes shamelessly
at each election for an Emperor in order to
obtain some political or material benefit, the
Electors of the Holy Empire held, with all
their strength, the instrument of their
influence and the mark of their dignity.
Those, among the princes, who disposed of
no share in the ballot which was to elect a
Cæsar, plotted in favor of the Electorate from
which they expected at least the maintainance
of their privileges and immunities.

Thus it happened that the German Emperor, elected as he was, enjoyed but a nomi-
nal authority, still lessened by traffic and
concessions, by the bribes paid at each turn
of the ballot. The oftener the elections were
held, the weaker became the Imperial authority.

All the better for the King of France, who
early considered himself a friend of these

Barons, of these prelates, of these burgher
Republics, all equally opposed to the Emperor's designs, and easy to divert from the
group of Teutonic forces.

And could the King of France have remained
apart from that other power which from outside joined its forces to those of the German
particularists in order to save the elective and
Republican character of the Empire? The
Pope, who had long been in dispute with
the Emperor, consequently found himself
in agreement with the King of France. This
community of interests soon brought about
a community of ideas.

" Secretly to hold Germany's affairs in the
greatest possible disturbance," this was the
sentence which was to be expressed, three
centuries later, by one of King Henri II's [1]
counsellors. That sentence, Philippe Auguste [2] had already traced it to himself,
while a pontiff, gifted with the most brilliant diplomatic genius, prepared against the
imperial power a plan which, in spite of

1. Son of Francis I (1519 † 1559).
2. 1165-1223.

an initial blunder, was bound to succeed.

The alliance between the King of France and Innocent III[1] resulted from no preconceived idea. The events had brought it about. In those centuries, which we have been taught to connect with mysticism and feelings, politics showed more self-possession, more calculation, less disinterestedness than we suppose. However, it was after several attempts were made in various directions that the policy of Paris and the policy of Rome joined on the same ground. Philippe Auguste, after having thought of the Imperial crown for himself, supported at first a candidate who was not the Pope's. The event proved that the King of France had been right, in driving back that Otto of Brunswick whose election was secured by the Holy See.

" Beware of that man, " said Philippe Auguste to the Pope, " you will see what a " reward you will receive from him for your " favors. "

1. Pope from 1198 to 1216.

The Capetian had serious reasons for apprehending the eventuality of a nephew of Jean Sans Terre (an ally of his great enemies, the Plantagenets), reigning over Germany. He was soon relieved when he saw Otto again starting the everlasting conflict of the Holy Empire against the Priesthood, going to war against the Papacy, and hardly crowned, invading St Peter's estates. Then Innocent III confessed that Philippe Auguste had been wise, that the King had been a good prophet and he asked for his help. The Capetian was little disposed to tax his army with that burden and contented himself by assuring the Holy See that there was no difference between their respective aims, and since then the two diplomacies acted in tune.

Against excommunicated Otto, Rome and Paris presented the same candidate to the Empire, Frederick [1], a Hohenstaufen, to tell the truth, but considered as harmless, on account of his young age. The supreme match was played on the battlefield of Bou-

1. 1194-1250.

vines, as Otto had understood that it was necessary to vanquish Philippe Auguste, in order to beat his rival and hit Innocent III. On running this chance for the sake of his kingdom, the Capetian did not neglect the force drawn from his alliance with the Pope. In high tones he boasted of it with his vassals, and strove to baffle the mind of his foe by claiming to be the champion of the Church and of the Faith. The victory threw the Golden Eagle and the Dragon, the Empire's symbols, into his hands. He lent them to Frederick whom Otto's defeat crowned Emperor, but the Emperor who was the most submitted to Rome, the most limited in his power ever seen.

The victory of Bouvines, result of a clever diplomacy, liberated France for many years from the Teutonic peril. It also marked the entrance of the French monarchy in the tournament of the great European policy.

Innocent III and Philippe Auguste had together secured the triumphant laurel. A Franco-Roman coalition had beaten the Imperial dominion. Thus, from experience, there arose a principle of European balance, entirely in favor of the French nation, and which through the centuries gave proof of its salutary effects. Rome and France were united by the same interests against a too strong Germany. And what was true in the xiii[th] century was true again in the xix[th]. Sedan is the counterpart to Bouvines. When the Pontifical power was upset, while there was no king to sit on the French throne, a hereditary German empire was seen proclaimed in the Palace of Versailles. Thus is forged the iron chain of the capital dates in our history.

Nearly a hundred years after Bouvines, the German problem presented itself again, and in almost identical terms to the French monarchy. But, during the xiii[th] century, the Capetian power had developed in the same proportion as the German power had declined. Philippe le Bel[1] (the Handsome), following up the policy of Philippe Auguste, with the benefit of the victory of 1214,[2] had no more to fear the scourge of an invasion. To the

1. 1268-1314.
2. Bouvines.

methodical enterprise of dividing and weakening the Empire which his predecessor had already started, he needed only to add the diplomatic ways and means.

Therefore, to the pretentions and the ultimatum of Adolf of Nassau[1], Philippe le Bel flatly answered with one word, which should enjoy a wider fame : " Too German. " The " Chronicle of Saint Denis " quotes this almost unknown anecdote and which all French children ought to be taught in school, in these ironic terms : " The King of France " having received this note, he summoned " his counsel in great solemnity and asked " what should be the reply. Then the mes- " sengers came back with the answer which " they tendered to their Lord (Alfred de " Nassau.) He broke the seal which was " of a huge size, and when the cover was " open, no other words were found in it " than : Too German. This reply had been " concerted over by the Earl Robert of " Artois with the King's Privy Council. "

1. Emperor of Germany in 1292-1298.

What could inspire such steadiness?   How did the Capetian dare to affect that spark's tone toward the Teutonic Emperor?   Because the King of France had developed and cemented his alliances with the Lords and cities of the Rhine, alliances which were the prelude of the celebrated league thanks to which Mazarin [1] succeeded later on in bringing the Rhenish populations under France's influence and control.

Philippe le Bel (the Handsome) had to mobilize an army neither against Adolf of Nassau nor against Albert of Austria [2].   His diplomats would suffice.   And when Albert died, the King of France continued the same policy presenting his own brother, Charles of Valois, as a candidate to the Imperial election.   Still, the crown fell to Henry of Luxembourg [3].   But by his education, his language, his habits, Henry was like one of our own princes and from his reign dates the

1. Italian Cardinal, endowed with French naturalization in 1639.   Prime Minister under Louis XIII and Louis XIV.
2. Emperor of Germany from 1298 to 1308.
3. Emperor of Germany from 1308 to 1313.

first epoch of the irradiation of France, of French customs, ideas and litterature over Germany.

The method of political and diplomatic action had proved efficient. The French royalty cared for no other, so far as Germany was concerned. In dealing with the German affairs our kings resorted to no other method until Charles V, that is to say till the very moment when a new situation was disclosed and the necessity made itself felt for an armed fight against the Austrian dynasty.

" No more than his predecessors, " writes an historian of the Middle Ages, " Philippe le Bel cared for an open war with the Empire; diplomatic proceedings had his favor ". The same held good with his successors until Francis the 1st [1]. Before the xvi[th] century, the wars between France and Germany were simple skirmishes. And when the day came to resort to arms, the lessons taught by the experience of centuries were not lost out of sight. Just in these circum-

1. Duke of Valois. Succeeded as King of France to his cousin Louis XII (1515).

stances the system of protection for the " German liberties " was fixed, a system warranting in fact the German anarchy and from which the ancient rule would no more depart.

The German anarchy of the past presents striking contrasts with that organisation, that discipline which is considered nowadays as the main aptitude of the Teutons. Some skepticism is allowed regarding the psychology of nations when one witnesses such a metamorphosis in a national temper. These transformations are to be explained only by the efficacity of the institutions. They are closely dependent on politics. Until the Hohenzollern's success, the history of Germany was a long struggle between the principle of authority and individualism, between Monarchy and the Republican spirit.

A strange mistake is prevalent about the men of former times when one supposes them better disposed than those of our times to bow before masters and to accept authority. In contrast to a common belief founded on ignorance, hereditary monarchy is a form of

Government much more frequent in modern days than in most other periods of history. It meets with much less opposition and resistance than formerly. In the Europe of the Middle Ages, the elective monarchies and even the Republics were equal, if not superior in number, to the royalties as we know them. It is well enough known that, in the past, Russia was Republican, and that, on the soil of autocracy, seven hundred years back, free institutions and the rule of partisanship were particularly flourishing. It is a grave mistake to suppose that mankind had to wait or 1789 in order to feel the flavour of freedom and chafe under tyranny's yoke. Almost everywhere, in Europe, till the xix[th] century, when, for the first time, royalty had settled in various countries and taken root without difficulty, one saw the nations reluctant towards hereditary monarchy, or but slowly used to it, sometimes caught by surprise, and sometimes, — this was the case with the Capetian monarchy, — welcoming it, in reward of its services.

The history of France, if we take it in the

x[th] century, until the election of Hugues Capet, affords a summary of the whole German history till the dawn of contemporary times. The Carolingians (heirs of Charles the Great) had werakened, their decadence had taken place much faster in France than in Germany. With us, the great feudatories had promptly endeavoured to use these circumstances in order to enervate and definitely ruin royal power by setting on the throne, in turns, a Carolingian and a Robertinian [1], with a view of preventing power from settling in the same family. When Hugues Capet took it in his hand, the same elements combined to check the future authority of his successors, with the hope of destroying it, as they had done with the Carolingian stem. Loyalty is not always the virtue of great Lords or of the aristocracies.

Hugues Capet and his offsprings were elected kings, like consuls for life, who, in order to elude the principle of election, had their eldest son crowned before their death,

1. An heir of Robert II, the Pious, Hughes Capet's son, king of France from 996 to 1031.

similarly as the German Emperors had their son called : King of the Romans. But the Archbishop of Reims had begun by refusing to Hugues Capet to anoint his son Robert the Pious " for fear that royalty should henceforth become an hereditary right... " Sentence full of meaning coming from a high ecclesiastic dignitary who lived about a thousand years ago. Only in the course of the xII[th] century, Louis VIII[1], father of Saint Louis[2], was the first Capetian who really had access to the throne by virtue of the hereditary principle and who was a King by inheritance, before he was by his coronation and the people's acclamation. A hundred years later, the " Salic law " will register that progress and victory of our Capetians. The maxim : " The King is dead : God save the King, " takes its place. Strange coincidence of history : this gain of heredity realized by the French royalty corresponds almost exactly, for Germany, to the great interregnum, which means the definite

1. King of France from 1223 to 1226.
2. King of France from 1226 to 1210.

decay of the powerful Hohenstaufen dynasty.

How explain this difference? How understand that the modest Capetians would succeed where these brilliant families of the
Ottos, the Henrys, the Fredericks, and, after
them, of the Habsburgs had lost the game,
in spite of their peerless shifts? Was it a
heavier task to build up the unity of Germany
than to construct that of France? Is it harder
to rule and command Germans than French?...
Everything taken in to account, there were
the same difficulties in forming a French
nation and a German nation, a French state
and a German state. The German people have,
true to say, their particularisms. But, we have
our partisanships. If the " German quarrel "
symbolizes their civil wars, we have our
factions in the Gaul's style which perpetuate
the fatal vice of division. Let us remember, in
the history of our country, the periods of
minorities, of regencies, the only weakness
of the hereditary monarchies. These eclipses
of the royal authority were always perilous,
always marked by an aggressive return of
anarchy. Since the minority of Saint Louis

until that of Louis XIV[1], one has seen, in our country, a renewal of seditions each time the reins of power were loosened. It is a ludicrous idea to suppose that our insurrectional uprisings and revolutions were born in 1789. A fameless but judicious author has written, in the first half of the last century, an original history of what he called " the six restaurations. " He quoted Louis IX, Jean le Bon[2] (after Étienne Marcel's conjuration), Charles VII[3], Henry IV[4] and Louis XIV reoccupying the throne in the same conditions as Louis XVIII[5]. There is something true in that view. And the " Cabochians[6], " the so-called league of public welfare, the century so dreadfully disturbed by the religious wars, are as many evidences that the French temper did not

1. Louis XIV, the Great, King of France from 1643 to 1715.
2. Jean II, King of France from 1350 to 1364. Son of Philippe VI.
3. Charles VII, King of France from 1422 to 1461. Restored to the throne by Jeanne d'Arc's rescue.
4. King of France, from 1589 to 1610.
5. King of France from 1814 to 1824.
6. A popular faction of the Burgundian party under Charles VI, named after its leader, a Paris, buscher.

impose to our kings an easier task than was that of the German Emperors. It is just as childish to interpret the history of our monarchy as an idyl which suddenly ended on the scaffold on January 21st 1793, as to fancy, as the revolutionary writers do, a French nation bent, during centuries, in obedience and who would have, hundred twenty five years ago, raised the head and, in conformity with M. Clemenceau's expression, waited till that moment " to clear up a long account with the principle of authority. "

The causes which had prevented, until nowadays, the hereditary monarchy to settle in Germany, are evident and simple. The great German interregnum lasted, according to a judicious remark, from 1250 until 1870. Why? The prospect of a great German monarchy was, for many people, and rightfully, a subject of awe... Numberless forces were always ready to join in order to hinder the formation of a Germany united and powerful under one sceptre only. " No king of Germany, " said the German princes. And this was the motto of the Kings of France too : " No king of Germany. " The interest of France was that there should be no hereditary chief assembling the Germanic masses. This idea was extremely clear with our political writers of the old time. Pierre Dubois (one of those " jurists " who occupied the place of great newspapermen and orators of nowadays, who were counsellors of the Government and leaders of the opinion), Pierre Dubois was peremptory in that respect. That pupil of St Thomas d'Aquin, that contemporary of Dante, expressed himself (we say it without exaggeration), as did Thiers himself in 1867... But, he did it pertinently. He feared Germany's unity for France which he considered as in direct relation with the rise, in the Teutonic countries, of a powerful royalty built up after the Capetian style. " For our sake, let us check that evil, " he concluded. Pierre Dubois was rightly admired by Renan who saw in him " a true statesman, " the first who clearly formulated " the principles in which, under all the great reigns, the crown of France found its guidance and rule. "

That conspiracy of the enemies of any strong and steady power in Germany, enemies at home, enemies abroad, had as effect to .cristallize the empire, for a sequence of years, in a pompous condition of anarchy. The Roman Holy Empire of Germanic stem has been described as : " a federative Republic under an Imperial presidency. " The very emperors who boasted of renewing Cæsar or Charles the Great, were only the elected presidents of that Republic and their characteraimed more and more at a simply decorative display.

In spite of all their efforts, in spite of their violences and tricks, the Emperors never succeeded in evading election. Sometimes they could reduce it to a mere formality. They never got its abolition. " The culminating point in the right of the Empire, " said the doctors of the German juridic science, " is considered as based on this : that the kings are not created by ties of blood, but by the vote of Princes. " In vain did the election of the Emperors depend only upon an insignificant number of voters, the principle of election had to bear its effects. There were but seven electors, the smallest electoral college ever seen. Still, the fruits of that suffrage so strictly reduced were the same which are imputed to universal suffrage in the democracies. It is an evident proof that election is pernicious in itself, and not by its modalities.

Electoral haggling, cabal, corruption, traffic of the bulletins of vote, not only all these common defects are to be found in the political customs of the Holy Empire, but these habits show, moreover, all the evils which in France the " district scrutiny " has been so often accused of, that is to say, the subordination of public interest to private ones to the bidders' shame. Each election was a rush of covetousnesses. With the electors, as with the elect, there were nothing but selfish calculations. Vainly the electors were called the seven mystic torches of the Holy Empire, or compared themselves to the seven lamps of the Apocalypse : they used their right of vote to impose their conditions to the candidates, to gain material benefits, if even

they did not make money of it. As to the
elected one, he was bound to act like an ordi-
nary candidate, before the ballot, that is to
say bound to promise or to give, he only
thought, once in possession of the mandate,
to compensate his sacrifices and to be re-
funded for his expenses. The Emperor, that
" half of Lord, " acted exactly like one of our
district deputies. The British historian, James
Bryce, who thoroughly studied the institutions and political customs of the Holy
Empire, has described in vehement terms
the results of the system of election applied
to the majestic suzerainty of those who pretended to be the rulers of Christian Europe.
" The electors, " says Bryce, " forced the
new elect to guarantee the maintenance of all
the privileges they were enjoying, including
the ones they had just extorted from him in
return for their votes ; they put him in a
hopeless impossibility to recover the land or
the rights he had lost ; they dared even to
depose their anointed Chief, Wenceslas of
Bohemia [1]. Thus handicapped, the Emperor

1. Wenceslas IV. Emperor in 1378.

only thought of reaping the largest possible benefit from his short contact with power, using his situation to raise his family and grow richer through the sale of the crown's lands and prerogatives. " Can a harder sentence be passed on a political system ? In one of its bushy, and' at first sight, so jumbled scenes of his second *Faust* which are like brief allegorical pictures of the history of mankind, Gœthe has ironically represented the Emperor and the grandees, calculating, each one for himself, under cover of a noble vocabulary, what profit they will draw from the ballot. James Bryce shows something more : that is that the elective monarchy " combination which has seduced, and will still seduce a certain class of political theoricians, " did not even yield to Germany the benefits one generally expects to derive from the designation of a chief by the majority of the votes. The elected one was neither the ablest nor the worthiest : in fact, the Imperial crown was in the hands of a small number of families who did their best to keep a hold on it. Ability, intrigue, contrivances, " politics " in the worst sense of the term, were substituted to merit, which was never taken into account.

Thus, after a few successes followed by reverses, the dynasty of the Habsburgs, from 1438 on and save for a short interval of five years in the xviii[th] century, was fortunate enough to keep the Imperial mandate, and to combine election with heredity. Likewise, in our Republican democracy, we saw seats of deputies transmitted from father to son.

But, the covetousnesses, the calculations, the interests of the elected were too conspicuous, his concessions to the elector too numerous and too shocking, The result was for the Imperial investiture to fall into the same discredit which nowadays in France affects the legislative. mandates. The Emperor, that " half of Lord, " suffered a diminution similar to the depreciation which our parliamentarians could not elude. The weakness, the increasing anarchy against which the Empire was struggling, were not the kind of causes able to endow the Emperors with the admiration and the gratitude of the people.

The elective monarchy, the life-presidency which, by turns, brought so many calamities to Poland, to Hungaria, to Bohemia, was not more beneficient towards Germany. They weakened her dreadfully, without bestowing that balance between authority and liberty which sometimes was the great argument in favour of that system and the basis for its partisans. The influences of the Crown, again says James Bryce, was not tempered, but destroyed. Each candidate was forced, in his turn, to buy his title with the sacrifice of rights owned by his predecessors, and, later on in his reign, was bound to return to the same shameful policy in order to secure his son's election. As he felt, at the same time, that his family could not sit solidly on the throne, he used it like a life-usufructuary does with his property, satisfied if he only draws from it the largest possible immediate gain. The electors, realising the strength of their position, availed themselves of and abused it.

Quite natural abuse; man is little inclined to respect the authority appointed and named by him. Therefore, Æneas Sylvius could, with some wit, say to the Germans : " In vain, you call the Emperor your King and your Lord. His title to reign is but precarious. He has no authority. You obey him just as muchas you please, and it pleases you very little. "

The greatest evil occurred the day when an Emperor, with praiseworthy intentions, thought he would save Germany from disorder, if only he could endow her with a Constitution. For, the Constitutionalist spirit does not, either. date from the xix[th] century. In 1356, Charles IV fancied in good faith that, by giving the Empire a chart, a fully-equipped document, he would endow it with peace and power. He had dreamed of putting an end to old contestations, by specifying once and for all the number and ability of the electors. In reality, he only settled the Empire in its troubles, he rendered the institution of an independent and strong monarchy impossible. Maximilian, who, a hundred and fifty years later, tried to react, to save Germany from rot, to give her back unity and power, had to strand on the Golden Bull.

" Never, " said he, " has a more pestilential pest raged over Germany. "

And, nowadays, a British historian, fond, as a Briton of Constitutional principles would be, might write about Charles IV : he legalized anarchy and called that building a Constitution [1].

There is an historic case, a hundred times illustrated in romance and in the theatre, and which shows the political customs of the Holy Empire as entirely similar to the electoral habits of all countries and all times. It

1. The Seven Princes, electors, acquired with the extension of their privileges, a marked and dangerous overbalance in Germany. They were authorized to enjoy in their States absolute and royal rights; their consent was indispensable for any public act of some importance. Soon, they got their ample share of that popular veneration which surrounded the Emperor, the same as of that effective power in which he was lacking. (Bryce.)

Likewise, we have witnessed in contemporary France the discredit of the Executive while the real authority passed into the hands of the electoral element.

is the famous election when Charles V
had Francis the 1st as a rival. Both being
Kings by divine right, the one in France, the
other in Spain, these gallant Knights, these
blossoms of chivalry.

Nevertheless, in their fight for the Imperial
crown, the same ways and means as a farrier
and a lawyer struggling for the same seat,
in one of our rural districts. The King of
France presented himself in the following
terms and supported this declaration of can-
didature with a manifest drawn by Cardinal
Duprat : " The King is largely endowed with
the gifts of genius, body and fortune, in full
youth, in full vigor, generous and therefore
beloved of his soldiers, able to endure vigil,
cold, hunger. But for the Catholic King[1],
one must realize his young age and that his
kingdoms are very distant from the Empire,
so that he would be unable to take care together of this and those. The customs of the
Spaniards are not at all similar, but thoroughly opposed to those of the Germans.

1. The King of Spain.

On the contrary, the French nation, almost on all points, resembles the German from whom she proceeds, that is to say from the Sicambers, as we are told by the ancient historians. "

To this the Habsburg replied that : " if he were not of true Germanic stem and birth, " he would not pretend to the Empire. He promised that, if he be elected, the German liberty " concerning the spiritual as well as the temporal, would not only be preserved, but extended. " While, if the King of France should become Emperor, he would hold the Germans under the same bondage as he did the French and deal with them at his pleasure. It is curious to see absolutism, the " old rule, " used as an argument by Charles the Vth against Francis the I[st], just as it would be by a radical candidate against a conservative. To strengthen the resemblance, there was even a desistance, that of Frederick of Saxony, whose votes went to Charles. Nevertheless, the latter's election had been secured at a heavy cost : a million ducats which he had been obliged to borrow.

In his drama : *Hernani*, Victor Hugo has personified in the King of Spain, the type of the eternal candidate when he puts on his lips the famous verses : " To be Emperor, oh rage, to miss it "... and further on : " I need three votes, Ricardo, what don't I need? " which are always at their place with the ambitious in full electoral fever.

It is easy to understand that with the Reform[1], the religious rivalries, the division of Germany into two camps (the Lutheran, and the Catholic) the supreme stroke had been inflicted upon the unity and the power of Germany. According to its well-established principle (to hold the German affairs in the greatest possible difficulty, as Marillac, Henry the II's favorite negotiator then said, the French monarchy took eagerly advantage of these circumstances. The kingdom was in the bitterest fight against the Emperor when it found allies in the persons of the Protestant princes. Spontaneously, these lords had looked towards the King of France

1. 1517.

and asked for his help against the Emperor
who aimed, they argued (such was their
Republican language), at the perpetual ensla-
vement of the German nation. So good an
opportunity was not missed. The Treaty
of Chambord was at once signed with the
Lutheran league. This Treaty beared, for
its title, and that title was a whole programme, *pro germania patriæ libertate recu-
peranda*, for the restoration of the Germanic
liberty, of which the King of France was
henceforth the official defender. Grandees
like Maurice of Saxony, free cities, like Strassburg and Nuremberg, were part of the
Treaty. The king of France bound himself
to support the Confederates against the
Emperor, to supply them with subsidies. In
exchange, they handed him Metz, Toul and
Verdun. This treaty signed, the Lutheran
League, strengthened by this alliance imposed on the Emperor, a few months later, the
Passau transaction by which Charles the V
renounced to restore any " Kingdom of
Germany. " Therein we see the model of the
cheap and safe operations with which the

French monarchy succeeded in averting the German peril, while she went on extending the limits of the national territory. It is hardly likely that, without this alliance with the German Lutherans, France would have got the better of the Austrian dynasty. The Empire, weakened and troubled within its boundaries, saw, at the same time, its estates go to pieces. France built herself, and reached her completion in proportion as Germany, or rather, as one then said, " The Germanics " progressed towards dissolution,

To fix and organize the German anarchy was to be the political masterpiece of the French xvii[th] century, to reward the labors and work of several generations and to mark the zenith of France, henceforth fearless facing her dangerous, but impotent and disarmed neighbour.

CHAPTER II

THE TREATIES OF WESTPHALIA : GERMAN
ANARCHY ORGANIZED
AND THE SECURITY OF FRANCE ASSURED

Sometimes we are led to believe that the
history of our country was not written by the
same race of men who furnished its material.
Our Kings, our Ministers, our great diplomats would be extremely surprised if they
could see how their work and aims were
construed in the minds of most of our historians, better suited, no doubt, for the writing
of romances and of lyric poetry, or for the
support of partisanship, than for anything else.
We have not in mind to assert that the old
French policy lacked any large and worldwide
conception, nor even in lofty imagination,

although some writers qualified it as too much " land-holder like. " In fact, the defence of the soil, the protection and the gradual increase of the national territory, formed the principal and permanent aim of the monarchy's programme. Cruel experiences were needed before our country could appreciate soundly a policy whose object was to withstand successfully these invasions which we have now suffered for the fifth time since the Revolution.

This was a permanent design throughout the struggle against the Austrian dynasty, a struggle which filled two centuries of our history, and which had to end in complete success. The main point was to prevent the Habsburgs from obtaining what the Hohenzollerns will gain in the xix[th] Century, that is to say : domination over all the Germanies. The object was to prevent Germany from realising her unity like France had realised her own. It was a matter-of-fact plan inspired by good sense and thoroughly led by the clear consciousness of the national interest. At the same time, humanity's civisation had to benefit by the result; for at the conclusion of the Thirty Years' War[1], when German power was broken for many years, Europe enjoyed one of its happiest periods. After the trials imposed upon the European world by Germanism in its full freedom, one must admire the wisdom of a policy which consisted in disarming Teutonic barbarity, in cutting down the monsters's claws.

With that policy, the French nation was nearly always in agreement from the depths of her soul. Sometimes, however, she thwarted or delayed its action. Later on, she damaged its results and almost entirely lost the signification of the scheme.

Thus, took place a ridiculous misrepresentation of the conceptions cherished by Henri IV[2] and whose realization was already on good way when the dagger of a fanatic put an end to the King's life. It has been asser-

1. 1618-1648. Started at Prague (Bohemia), when the authorities were thrown out of the windows of the Hradschin Castle.

2. King of France from 1589 to 1610. Chief of the Branch of the Valois-Bourbons.

led, in recent times, that Henri IV anticipated the policy of the Revolution and the Napoleons; that he planned the partition of Europe, according to the principle of nationalities. Thanks be to God that the theory did not go so far as to assume that he had begun that immense enterprise, elaborated for eight years with his minister Sully, by a mere compliance with a love passion. The truth is that, as a Bourbon, he was reviving the plan of the Valois, lost out of sight during the civil war and anarchy to which his coronation put an end. Henri IV schemed what was to be realized under the following reign by Richelieu : the downfall of the Austrian dynasty. But his death, the minority of his son, the end of beneficent dictatorship led France into a new Republican stage. For another period, divisions, and private interests prevailed. France will have to wait until Louis XIII[1] has become a man, until he may champion a great Statesman with his authority, to see the factions punished, partisanship reduced to

1. Son of Henri IV, 1601-1643.

impotence, and the national interests restored to preeminence. Anarchy corresponding to periods of weakness and decay, royal dictatorship corresponding to periods of interior revival and expansion, we venture to say that this alternance is the key-note of our whole history.

The grave disorders which marked Louis XIII's minority reflected detrimentally upon German affairs. In the year 1620, when France's situation was in the utmost perturbation, when intrigues were raging, a deep sea-wave proceeding (as it has done so often in our history, as it has done again in 1914), from the limits of Central and Oriental Europe, imposed on the French rulers the necessity of facing the foreign scourge. How far, indeed, from us, from the country where so much covetousness, so many parties and ambitions were fighting against each other, when our Protestants were ready to proclaim the " Republic of Reform," how far was this Bohemia who attempted to reconquer her independence and rose against her Emperor! Still, one had to deal with her. The foreign policy ruled France again, caught her at the very moment when the French were much more disposed to indulge in their private quarrels than to consider the other side of the frontier. In that respect the episode of the *defenestration*[1] at Prague, which opened the Thirty Years War, recalls by its consequences the murder at Serajevo!

The Czech nationalists at that moment, whose attempt at liberation was embittered by a religious upheaval, had chosen the Palatine Elector as their chief and received help from the reformed princes of the Empire. The German affairs were started again and in the same conditions as they had been in the preceding century, at the time of the struggle against Charles V. Rising against the Emperor, the German Protestants applied for support to their natural and traditional ally, the King of France, protector of German liberties. The duke of Bouillon was deputed to bring the request to Paris.

But, many things had changed since Henri's

---

1. First episode of the Thirty Years War.

murder (1610). During the great disorders which followed his death, the leading principles of the French policy had been lost sight of; a reconcilement had taken place with Austria, sealed by Louis XIII's marriage. Emperor Ferdinand did not overlook so good an opportunity. At the time when the Protestants were sending their delegates to the Court of ·France, he dispatched an Ambassador, Furstenberg, commissioned to plead that the King's cause and the Emperor's cause were the same. The arguments developed by Furstenberg were strikingly modern. The Ambassador of Ferdinand II represented to Louis XIII and to Luynes[1] that, with the Palatine Elector's rebellion, the matter was, in fact, that of a Republican plot, that, from all the Republics, free cities, aristocracies and democracies, a movement had arosen threatening all the monarchies alike. From Switzerland, from Holland, from the Hanseatic cities, he pointed out, the Revolution was gaining ground, rallying even those Catholic

---

1. Charles d'Albert de Luynes, favorite of Louis XIII.

cities of Germany where the " plural government " was ruling. And, quite cleverly,
Furstenberg suggested to the King of France to
carefully watch his own Protestants, always on
the verge of, or in a state of insurrection, Republicans and Separatists, at the same time very
dangerous for the authority of the Sovereign
and for the unity of the Kingdom. " What
are these people's pretentions? Are they
not just like those of our's? " exclaimed the
skilful diplomat. " Did they not plot together, hold secret assemblies and collect
money in order to put in danger, if they
could, the realm of France and undermine
the power of the King. " Should Louis XIII
intervene in favor of the Protestants in Germany, he would encourage his own Huguenots
and never get rid of them anymore. " " Who
supports the rebels, teaches rebellion to his
own subjects? Whoever listens to the forei-
gners, when they charge their magistrate (their
government), opens the door to sedition at
home, and if you assist the insurgents against
their Kings, these, after beating their own
Lords, will turn your people against yourself..."

Furstenberg sustained eloquently the thesis of the solidarity between the thrones, which after all, is in no way more deceptive than the thesis of the solidarity between the liberal powers and the democracies. Still, in one sense, his arguments hit the mark. At the very moment he was speaking, the Protestant peril was very serious for France. To favor it, by supporting the cause of the Reformation in Germany, would have been dangerous.

Richelieu[1] himself, having the masterhood, will begin his work by breaking Protestantism as a political power before starting with an exterior action and with a renewal of the French policy in Germany, according to the ascertained principle of the past. The European work of Richelieu had to be preceded by a period of dictatorship, of cleansing and of restoration of order at home.

Even without looking for historical comparisons, they come obviously to our mind, by the simple evidence of facts. France has not ceased to be in the same geographical site, to

1. Armand Jean du Plessis, cardinal de Richelieu, 1585 + 1642.

be surrounded by the same neighbours, to occupy the same position in regard to European problems. Now, in similar cases, the same actions determine the same consequences. Louis XIII was not influenced by Furstenberg's brilliant arguments to bestow on the Emperor the help of his arms : but he kept, at least, neutral, as Napoleon III did in 1866. As then, too, the awakening was painful. One has often quoted the " thunder-bolt " of Sadova. This metaphor applies exactly to the battle of the White Mountain.

When the King of Bohemia was beaten by Ferdinand's armies, everyone understood that the Emperor had obtained a great increase of power and that the peril of the Austrian dynasty was again in sight. The Ambassadors and ministers of the King, in Germany, sent the most urgent messages to Paris. They represented that the line followed in maintaining neutrality, without supporting Bohemia and the Protestant League against the Emperor, had been wrong. Referring to the " raison d'État, " and for the sake of France, they recommended a change of policy. They asserted it was necessary not to be deceived by a so-called plan of counter-reformation as exhibited by the Emperor, and that, under the pretence of restoring the unity of creed in Germany, Ferdinand was simply plotting to restore political unity.

That manifesto of the Ambassadors was a complete lesson in high diplomacy : if our country ever lacked in anything, it never was in sound counsellors or far-seeing minds. What was sometimes wanting were governments ready to recognize their errors and return to the correct line of action. In 1866, Napoleon III had, also, at his service, a good diplomat, who attempted to make amends for the blunder. Drouyn de Lhuys was not listened to, and the elected Chief of the Imperial democracy even boasted of the neutrality he had unwisely observed. In 1620, however, the mistake committed under similar conditions, save that, instead of proceeding from wrong principles, it derived from a misconception of interests, was redeemed without delay. This ability to make use of every lesson, to adapt oneself to events, characterizes the general work of the Capetian monarchy, that is to say the creation of France, the conservation and development of the results gathered in the course of that great journey, fruitful in ever-renewed surprises, which covers the history of a country like our's.

It was to the impression stamped in Louis XIII's mind by the " thunder-bolt " of the White Mountain[1] that Richelieu owed his influence over the King. He received all the authority he wanted to perform his great scheme of European policy. When order had been restored by severe means, amongst which the scaffold played its part, the Huguenot state having been broken, Richelieu could freely turn towards German affairs. La Rochelle[2], the capital of the Protestant Republic, being taken, the Cardinal was enabled to contract an alliance against the Austrian dynasty with Gustavus Adolphus[3] who had

---

1. Battle of the White Mountain (1620). Defeat of Frederick Palatine Elector, King of Bohemia.
2. French port on the Atlantic.
3. King of Sweden 1594-1632.

just appeared on German soil as the champion of the Reform.

Richelieu's policy reproduces, with striking similarity, the main lines of the Capetian policy in former centuries. The Cardinal, too, did his best in order to avoid resorting to arms so long as something was to be expected from diplomacy. He allowed the Danes first, then the Swedes to fight and wear the Emperor out, before he permitted French blood to be spilled. Then, through diplomacy, he prepared the success of armed intervention. At the diet of Ratisbonne, where the work of his agents checked the Emperor, his plan was in tune with the motto formulated under Henri II, but brought in to practice long before that prince : " to maintain German affairs in the greatest possible condition of uneasiness. "

To that policy, schemed in the foregoing century, Richelieu added a new element which gave it new scope. The attitude which he had been forced to adopt towards Protestantism as a result of the Revolutionary and separatist plot of the French Huguenots, had introduced some modifications into our alliance with the Protestants of Germany. The problem to be solved was, indeed, a complex one. The interests of France were on the side of the German Evangelic League and of Gustavus Adolphus, the hero of Reform, against the Emperor. But it was impossible, considering the position assumed by the Protestant party in France, to fraternize, without a counterpart, with European Protestantism. Such was the view which the confidential auxiliary of the Cardinal, the celebrated Father Joseph, expressed in striking terms when speaking of the alliance with the German Protestants. He said that : " One had to use these things like a remedy which, in a small dose, is an antidote, and of which too much is mortal. "

Arising from two necessities, born of the obligation for adjusting interior and exterior interests, Richelieu's policy, instead of being overburdened by the difficulty, received an increase of energy therefrom. While assisting the Protestant League in Germany, he conceived the idea of separating the cause of the

Emperor from the Catholic causes. Convinced that the Catholic princes were just as fond of their independence from the Empire, as were the Protestant princes or States, he displayed all his efforts in impressing their minds that the Counter-Reformation, which officially was the aim of Ferdinand III, was only a pretence covering a plan for the subjection of Germany under the Habsburgs. Richelieu, in his quality as Prince of the Church, and his best agent, Father Joseph, in his quality as Capuchin Friar, were entitled to speak in that sense. They resorted effectually to the policy of Ferdinand III himself, making use of Catholic ideas and feelings in Germany, in the same manner as they had been worked out by the Emperor himself, in order to extend the influence of the King of France, in his quality as " protector of the German liberties." While the Habsburg laid his chances on a single card, Richelieu managed his game so that France should appear, on the contrary, like a disinterested peacemaker, and as the equitable recourse for everyone who had some grievance at hand. In one word, the Bourbon presented himself as an umpire in a claim where the Habsburg was only a party.

The acutest historian for that period, M. Gustave Fagniez, in his magisterial book on Father Joseph, has pointed out the practical sense running through all this part of Richelieu's diplomacy. Neither as a statesman was Richelieu disposed to work blindly for the cause of Protestantism, nor as a Churchman was he ready to be deceived by the dignified appearance of the Counter-Reformation. " Infact, " said M. Gustave Fagniez, " between France and the Evangelical party, there was only the bond which results from parallel actions against a common foe. In spite of the real strength which our subsidies, as well as the hope to have us as partners in the fray, had bestowed on the Protestant coalition, Richelieu cared much less to bring together and encourage the members of that coalition than to break up the group of the Catholic States which, in Germany as in Italy, gathered round the Austrian dynasty, and to draw them under France's patronage and shield. His real predilections, his sympathies were with the German Catholic party and its chief (Maximilian, Duke of Bavaria); there lies the main-spring of his policy. "

Richelieu had refused to assist the confessional interests of Protestantism; he had declined all propositions of adhesion to the Protestant League of the Hague. In a word, he had been true to his understanding with the German Protestants in the limits traced by France's interest. Likewise, he firmly opposed any attempt to draw him into a Catholic League, or to induce him to give up the particular contracts of France with such or such a Reformed State. He never admitted the idea that a European conflict could be limited " to the conflict between two religions. " His choice went to a " third party " which would defend the independence of Central Europe and constitute, against the formation of a great German monarchy, an impassable barrier. If, instead of the Catholic Habsburgs, Richelieu's policy, in this century, would have had to face the Protestant Hohenzollerns, it would have been applied in the same way and would have coincided on all points.

This policy was crowned when the most important of the Catholic princes, the Elector of Bavaria, Maximilian, met the Cardinal's views. Henceforth, there was no fear anymore that either German or European Catholicism would be enslaved by the Austrian House. The Holy See itself gave its adhesion to the " third party. " The formula of the European balance, that is to say, of the independence of the European states from the German Empire, was ascertained. Of that independence of the nations, which was the fruit of her efficient work, France was naturally the champion. But one sees now to what extent the commission of the King of France, as " protector of the German liberties " had progressed. Instead of an ally, an inciter of the rebels, he became the impartial guardian, the feeble's friend and champion; whether Catholics or Protestants, his justice was extended to all. Still, the Catholic populations, the most in touch with our country, the most Latinized, too, the casiest, consequently, to assimilate, entered into our friendship, we dare even say, under our protectorate : these good relations were to last until 1870.   The League of the Rhine, which Cardinal Mazarin[1] founded a short time later, made of the Rhine provinces and of Southern Germany, a kind of outpost of the French Kingdom.   They were allies who, in the future, would act like a rampart against the ever-threatening advance of the more remote and more barbarous German tribes, and, in the meantime, they would welcome the pacific penetration of our ideas and habits.   The limits of our frontier up to the banks of the Rhine, would then take place, safely and without damage.   The operation could only entail benefit to all.

Thirty years of war were necessary, in the xvii[th] century, in order to ruin the Imperial power, that is to say, to beat Germany.   But she was beaten to such a degree that the vanquishers could dispose of her at their will.   And it took her less time to reco-

____

1. Giulio Mazarini. Italian Cardinal; 1602-1661.

ver from her material damages than to rise
from the political decay to which she had
been chained.

Richelieu had died before he could see the
crowning of his work. But the principles
of his policy were so well anchored and in
such solid ground, and in such a manner,
that his disappearance changed nothing to
the affairs in hand. An Ambassador of
the Republic of Venice, where diplomatic
experience was so advanced, wrote to his government, after the great Cardinal's death :
" One can assert that, after having upset the
Empire, troubled England, weakened Spain,
Richelieu was the instrument chosen by Pro-
vidence to lead the main events of Europe. "

This overthrow of the Empire, which was
the result aimed at by French policy for many
years, was secured by the celebrated Treaties
of Westphalia[1]. There was no need for any
innovation, nor even of any imaginative
strain. The French peace, which Germany
received without sorrow — and there lies

1. 1648. Closing the Thirty Years War.

the superiority of the art, — rested on experimental notions, and was only the development of political principles whose beneficial
efficiency had been thoroughly acknowledged
in the past. The Treaties of Westphalia,
model of every serious and lasting peace with
the German countries, included four elements harmoniously combined in order to
prevent Germany from becoming again a
great state dangerous for France and for
Europe. These elements were : territorial
and political parcelling; elective basis of the
supreme power; parliamentary rule; and the
guarantee of the vanquishers for the maintainance and the respect of the whole system.

Territorial parcelling, which was ascertained by a judicious use of German particularism, was brought to its extreme limit.
Where was the Emperor who pretended to
divide Germany into ten circles, each of
them with a Governor? Henceforth, there
were to be two thousand enclosures (Principalities, Republics, Bishoprics, Margraviates
or simple commanderies), among which more
than two hundred were Sovereign States with

regal rights and able, above all, to contract alliances according to their fancy. Germany was hashed into small pieces, disjointed, dislocated. She presented the appearance of a variegated patchwork, as, nowadays, one of the Chancellors of the United Empire, prince von Bülow, was to say. Around a few Electorates of substantial size, there was a bunch of principalities and free cities, something like Monaco, Liechtenstein, Saint-Marin, the republic of Andorra, multiplied to hundreds of examples. Germany, at that degree of dispersion, was called : '' the puzzle of the geographer ''. The geographers themselves were at a loss and lacked colors to distinguish all these numerous territories.

However, on leaning over that whimsical map, one discovers that this disorder, where nothing had been left to chance, was an effect of political foresight and art. Facing the hereditary estates of the Austrian House, three Electorates of an average size : Bavaria, Saxony and Brandenburg, are put as sentinels. On France's side, on the contrary, the way remains quite open. On the Rhine :

not one State of some power or extent. Moreover, the Treaties provided that not one among the numberless little dynasties should dispose of more forces than its neighbour. Exceptional circumstances are to arise before Prussia will break the meshes of that net. In each of the Princely branches the treaty maintains rivalries and competitions. There are Hohenzollerns, Wittelsbachs, Wettins, Guelfs, etc. who reign on all sides and watch over each other from everywhere. The plan was so successful that the two branches of the House of Brunswick, in dispute ever since that time, were only reconciled in our time.

The trial complained of by the geographers was above all painful for the Emperors themselves, against whom, according to a strong and happy expression of Mignet, the Empire had been henceforth edified, and who were obliged to give up any hope of adjusting and bringing its scattered members into action. In that dislocated Germany everyone enjoyed his independence, and could follow his fancy without the slightest care for the interests of the commonwealth. When La Fontaine[1] said : " The smallest Prince has his Ambassadors, " he was alluding to those German princelets who were enabled to contract any alliance at their choice. In the 1914 war, we saw the principality of Liechtenstein declare her neutrality and refuse her military contingents to Austria. Two hundred Liechtensteins of all sizes enjoyed the same freedom in Germany, parcelled as she had been by the authors of the Westphalian Treaties. Upon German particularism, upon private interests and competitions, upon the pride of the German princes and clans, they had laid the foundation of an inextricable system in which Germany, as a nation, seemed entangled forever.

From the Emperor there was nothing to expect for the awakening of the national feeling. His prestige emerged from the Münster and Osnabrück Congresses[2] more damaged than ever. The Austrian dynasty

1. French poet, 1621-1695.
2. The preliminaries of the Westphalian treaties were signed at Münster and Osnabrück.

had not subdued the Protestants, she had lost her influence over the Catholics, she remained submitted to election while the Electors had grown in strength. And if she succeeded in keeping the Imperial title until the Holy Empire's downfall, it was only thanks to concessions and sacrifices of power still more burdensome after each scrutiny. The election of Leopold I, which followed the conclusion of the Treaties, was a real scandal. France interfered openly and the envoys of the King at Frankfort, Grammont and Hugues de Lyonne, without any mystery, bought the Electors who did not hesitate to sell their votes at auction : we should say, that they behaved just like the politicians shamelessly bribed in our modern times. Mazarin complained bitterly of their exactions : " Although it might be advantageous, " he said, " to let the world believe that there is still a large stock of money in France, because that supposition is, in a selfish age, the most influential to win the world over to His Majesty's friendship; there are reasons good enough, without diminishing

His Majesty's credit, for persuadnig everyone to use restraint in his pretentions, on account of present circumstances. ''

Through these ways and dealings, the King of France disposed of more power in the Empire than the Emperor himself. Grammont and Lyonne obtained this from Leopold I, a capitulation by which he bound himself, among other obligations, to give up all interest in the Netherlands, in the Franche-Comté, to separate from Spain, etc. The election allowed France to deal with the Empire as our interests commanded.

Elected at Frankfort, residing in Vienna, the poor Emperors had, moreover, to face a Parliament sitting in Ratisbonne, and with which they shared the rests of a broken and precarious authority. The institution of the Empire's Diet, of which the Reichstag is the direct offspring, was nothing new. The Diet traced its origin as far back as the very origin of Germany : an article of the Osnabrück treaty had only to extend its former attributions. Let us suppose that, after the 1914 conflagration, the Allies, winning the war, may decide, for instance, that the Reichstag will be entitled to overthrow the Ministries, and that each one of the States represented in the federal Council will enjoy an individual vote, instead of leaving the plurality of the votes to Prussia : this would be exactly the way by which France, in the xvii[th] century, succeeded in endowing Germany with a liberal constitution, the best fitted for the maintainance of division.

It is surprising that writers should have ascribed the origin of the parliamentary system to the xviii[th] century when one considers the dexterity (proving a direct knowledge of the life of the Assemblies) with which our diplomacy disposed the wheelworks of the Diet, in order to shackle any strong Government which might raise its head in Germany. The composition of that Court was skilfully intricate. Electors, princes, cities, each group forming a college, it was reasonable to rely upon the interests and feelings of these three bodies, generally united against the Emperor, but divided on the rest, to keep them quarrelling among each other. The Diet reproduced all the territorial, political and religious divisions of Germany and stewed them in a closed pot. The cities, above all, represented the democratic element. Mazarin notes with satisfaction : '' Hamburg, not tospeak of the others, has declared that the Diet still breathed the air of ancient German liberty. '' Very strict and minute regulations concerning the debates and the proceedings of the scrutiny, working under the pretext of a protection for each member's rights, rendered the despatching of affairs desperately slow, and sometimes made every solution impossible.

Moreover, by the program of its attributions, the Diet had to face the most arduous of solutions, the thorniest of problems, each of which was bound to raise disputes and conflicts, particularly in regard of finances and taxes. According to the forecast of its French advisers, the Diet was the conservatory of German dissension. '' What are they doing there, but quibbling and wrangling like schoolmasters? '' exclaimed Leibniz[1]. Ano-

1. German philosopher born at Leipzig (1646-1716).

ther political German writer of the same period, said ironically of the Parliament of Ratisbonne : " It would be a curious thing to discover what so many deputies at the Diet have accomplished for so many years, and what was the use of so many state dinners, of so much Spanish wine swallowed in the morning, of so much Rhine wine swallowed at night. The truth is that they handle an inextricable business and that, after their long and hopeless striving, they can only boast that they did not keep their arms folded. "

Other Germans, — very few indeed, — keeping a gleam of patriotism alive, and a certain sense of the nation's interests, deplored that fatal parliamentary system which, a one of them remarked " plunged Germany in perpetual night. " Indeed, as had been observed by an historian " the foreigner, at once, tried to derive profit from the vices of the institutions with the connivance of the interested parties. "

The King of France had secured the right, — abnormal, indeed, — of being represented

at the Diet of the Empire by a plenipotentiary
whose true mission was to watch the Assembly's works, to secure sympathies among its
members, and to turn its discussions in favor
of the French State's interest. The collec-
tion of the diplomatic instructions given, under
the old rule, to our ministers at the German
Diet, is, from that point of view, very significant. The aim is to use the German parliamentary system in the interest of France.
Along this line our diplomacy had neither a
scruple nor a doubt. In 1698, for instance, it
was feared in Paris, that the Diet would
grant some increase of his military forces to
the Emperor. M. Rousseau de Chamoy received
the following directions : " The deliberations
of the Diet at Ratisbonne about the most
important affairs are generally hampered by
incidents of so little weight that it will
depend upon M. de Chamoy's skill to take
advantage of these various incidents in order
to turn off, as far as possible, the debates
regarding the armaments, without showing,
however, the slightest concern for the question. With that in view, he will avoid star-

ting any discussion on the matter; but, at the first opportunity he will, in a natural way, handle, with the delegates of the Princes of the Empire, topics of some interest for their Lords, and he may, on the excuse of showing them, for their proper advantage, the utility of, or the objections to, these armaments, demonstrate that they have, at present, nothing to fear from his Majesty.

"But he shall use these arguments without any insistance, and, as His Majesty trusts that he will most carefully observe the fluctuatious in the Diet, he shall find auspicious circumstances to discard, through the simple intricacy of the affairs to come, any proposition susceptible of impeding the maintainance of peace."

Our great-nephews will probably hear of similar instructions given by Wilhelm II to his Ambassadors in Paris, in order to check the vote of military budgets in our parliament. To secure partisans in the Diet at Ratisbonne became the early aim of French diplomacy, a tradition faithfully continued by "the Cabinet's academicians." In 1726, Chavigny carried with him, on his way to Ratisbonne, these wittily discreet recommendations : " He shall fully meet His Majesty's views, if he gains the confidence of the principal ministers of this Assembly in a sufficient degree to be informed of every thing, and make use of the opportunities he may have at hand to hasten, to delay or to prevent, through seasonable advice, the various resolutions on the tapis according to their conformity or opposition with his Majesty's purposes. Of course, he shall strictly avoid showing any responsibility in the turn of events, for, the origin being discovered, a contrary effect would ensue. "

It would be strictly improper that the plenipotentiary of France should be charged, at Ratisbonne, " with fomenting the division which is already so noticeable in the Empire. " In fact, he does not occupy his post for any other purpose. He goes there in order to favor German discord and prevent any harm being done to the system established by the Treaty of Westphalia. By a supreme precaution crowning the work, the king of

France has called himself the trustee of the Treaties of 1648. By him this German Charter which, as we must bear in mind, is also the Charter of Europe, is declared beyond attaint. Whoever tampers with it will have to deal with his justice.

First shared with Sweden (which, during the xvii[th] century, played the part devolved nowadays to Russia), the guarantee of the Treaties of Westphalia soon belonged to France alone. In that respect, the monarchy did not slacken one single moment. Having succeeded in dividing and in disarming Germany, it did not want to have the old state of things revived in any way, nor to see the result of the efforts accomplished by the French nation put in question again. In 1788, at the eve of the Revolution, in sight of the Prussian encroachments on Germany, the Government of Louis XVI still claimed the rights and the duties of France, as the traditional guarantee of German liberty.

The masterpiece of the Westphalian system was perhaps that the Germans themselves showed their satisfaction with it, so true was

it that it answered to their nature and tastes.
In vain, the Emperor Ferdinand III, through
the pen of his writers, who then held the part
of our present officious newspaper-men, told his
people that the King of France, instead of
working for their rights, had worked only for
himself, and that the Bourbon aimed at the
tutorship of the Germanies reduced to
division and impotence. Did the Emperor
ever mingle with French affairs, encourage
the " Frondes, " or encourage the Parlia-
ments? And, further, he demonstrated that,
under the pretence of the German liberties,
the Kings of France snatch, one after the
other, pieces from the Holy Empire : yes-
terday the bishoprics, to-day Alsace, to-morrow Lorraine, or anything in the same
style. The Germans kept cool under these
lessons. They were satisfied with their dis-
sensions. More, they were proud of it. This
Constitution, which they owed to the foreigner and which the French policy had
matured, they discovered that it bore a
national stamp. Their jurists made long
commentaries about it and did not fail to

find its origin in the customs of the ancient Germans. They exhausted themselves in learned definitions, after which they happened, like Puffendorf in the xvii[th] century, to conclude in these terms : " There is nothing else to say, but that Germany is an abnormal body, which, so far as policy is concerned, looks like a monster (*monstro simile*). From a regular Kingdom, she degenerated and has fallen into a form of government so badly combined that she is no more a monarchy, although she presents some appearance of it, nor a whole or a system of various confederated States, but rather something wavering between these two regimens ".

This is what Voltaire[1] with his usual wit, sums up in two lines : " The name of the Holy Empire still survived. But the difficulty was to determine what Germany was and what that Holy Empire was also. " However, the definition had been delivered, from the first day, when Oxenstiern spoke of a " *confusio*

1. 1694=1778.

divinitus conservata, " a confusion kept under with master-hand. This hand was that of the foreigner.

Strange to say : the Germans did not realize the facts in their proper time and have only understood recently that the solicitude shown by France for the liberties of Germany was a precaution taken to shield her own.

* *
*

Though beneficial for France, inasmuch as it seemed to prevent the German peril for ever, and, in fact, spared her, until 1792, the evil of invasions, the Treaty of Westphalia did not limit itself to the conception of the immediate or, better, of the selfish interests of our country. What gave a peculiar solidity to the basis of that audacious political construction was that it proceeded from a general principle involving for the future the whole of Europe's interests. How strange it sounds to hear the heirs of the Revolutionaries, who destroyed the diplomatic work of the monarchy, complaining of and storming against the ambitions of the new German Empire and claiming for an international rule under which the independence of the small and middle States would be respected! Their impatience at rebuilding what the Revolution has destroyed, means the confession of a century's long error.

All the measures to which the fancy of our publicists, often in the most absurd and inefficient way, is resorting to in order to protect the world against the German scourge, had been put in motion by the Westphalian Treaty. *Plurality of the States :* this on the principle of balance which excludes universal monarchy. *Independence of the States :* no possible abuse of force against the weak. *Right of intervention* against the public burglars who violate or threaten to violate the European public law. France, in the name of that right, could assume the action of a preventive policeman for the sake of the common security. And she could act that way, without harm or peril, because she was the first interested in the maintenance of a state of things in which she was also the first by her power and wealth. Thus, the French policy had succeeded, in the middle of the xvii[th] century, in rendering Europe more or less habitable, in saving her from the *Faustrecht,* from the barbarous right of the fist, from the rude conceptions spread, a thousand years earlier, by the German invasions.

Since the Roman peace, since the failure of the Christian Republic, the civilized world could, for the first time, breathe and live in tranquillity. Thanks to the European system founded upon Germany's impotence by the Treaty of Westphalia, the ancient world has enjoyed a rest of a hundred and fifty years. A relative rest, of course, but which still appears as a golden age when compared to the following period, a period of war between the nations and of huge slaughters among mankind. All the aspirations, only more acute since the 1914 conflagration, for the protection of Europe against Germany, aim at some restoration of the Westphalian Treaty, which the French monarchy had declared beyond attaint and about which, Proudhon said strikingly that, « it stands forever », in favor of European society, because it answers to its essential needs, like the eternal laws presiding over all the human societies whose life would be impossible without the respect of contracts and without the protection of the feeble against the whim of the stronger.

Proudhon [1], who has, in the midst of his vagaries, often shown the clearest comprehension of realities, has very well pointed out, in his pamphlet, *If the Treaties of 1915 are no more*, the character of the 1648 Treaties, which he called the best possible adjustment for Europe, the safest shield against the abuses of force. Except for a certain element metaphysics which his mind could never drop entirely, Proudhon's remark has great weight at a moment when the question again arises to ascertain for the nations, with the guarantee of their liberties and existence, the regulating principle of their intercourse.

" The Treaty of Westphalia, " writes

1. French philosopher (1809-1865).

Proudhon, « has recognized, in opposition with the ideas which, since time immemorial, prevailed in the world, not that the right of war, then in full application, was a chimera, a prejudice of barbarity : nobody would have been convinced of it. It declared this only, that the scheme of a universal monarchy, extreme consequence of the right of war, admitted by the ancient societies, was chimerical ; that, therefore, whatever might be the wars which in the future might afflict the Christian nations, these wars never could absorb them all in one only, and thus renew the experience of a unique State; that, provided an adequate map be made for their respective territories, the plurality of the powers was, for the future, registered as a wise basis, and so far as possible, ought to be maintained by means of their equality or mutual balance.

'' Since that time, the principle of mutual balance has been inscribed in the Rights of Nations ; so that one can safely say, in full truth and logic, that if the right of victory, or the prevalence of force is the first article in the Rights of Nations, the plurality of powers, and, consequently, the system of balance, is the second.

" As long as there will be a plurality of powers balancing each other more or less, the Treaty of Westphalia exists ; one chance only remains to efface it from Europe's public law, and that is to change Europe again into a unique Empire. Charles V and Napoleon failed in their attempt; we venture to say, after that double failure, that unity and concentration, to such a degree, are in opposition with the fate of nations; the Treaty of Westphalia, superior expression of a justice identified with the force of things, lasts for ever. "

From the absolute standpoint which he adopts, Proudhon overlooks only two considerations which he certainly would have welcomed, had he witnessed the 1870 and 1914 wars and Germanism in its full fury. The first is that this very justice was founded upon Germany's weakness; the second, that this very justice concorded with France's welfare.

That European system, such as it was built up by the Westphalian Treaties, France was bound to champion. Any disturbance striking that system would hit France at the same time. Our European policy, therefore, had to be, for the future, a conservative policy. Of course, nobody could seriously believe that Europe would remain crystallized in the form devised in 1648. Changes were unavoidable in the course of ages. New problems had to arise. Nevertheless, it should at least have been possible to solve them in the spirit of our classical diplomacy and according to the principles laid down by the monarchy and by the eminent counsellors of the crown. To reject the lessons of experience and the results already secured, under the pretext of constructing Europe on another basis and of endowing her with a new organization, such foolishness could turn only to some competitor's profit, deprive France of the privilege of her primacy, and put again in question, not only the balance and the public rights of the ancient commonwealth, but the very existence of our nation. This blunder is precisely the one commited by the Revolution.

We shall see how the French people, after securing the auspicious conditions of their peace and greatness, thanks to their hereditary guides and to their illustrious statesmen, have done their best to destroy, with their own hands, all they had constructed to bring the world back to the age of iron and barbarity, while ingenuously aiming at the regeneration of mankind.

CHAPTER III

" Louis XIV, " said Sainte-Beuve[1], " had only good sense, but hehad a lot of it. " Louis XIV showed that good sense when he reproached Louvois with the great blunder of having ordered the ravages in the Palatinate. Nothing, indeed, more than violence was in disagreement with the policy which the King intended to follow towards the German countries. That policy corresponded exactly to what has been called nowadays : " pacific penetration. "

What a difference between the Germans such as they appeared from the middle of the

---

1. Celebrated French writer (1804-1869).

xvii[th] until the end of the xviii[th] century and their appearance to-day ! Just as tractable they then were, eager to be schooled by us, to adopt our customs and speak our language, just as stiff, unsociable, proud of their " Kultur, " intoxicated by the superiority of their race they stand before us to day. The " Germanies " from 1650 onward were a sort of province, where the people spoke a rough country-dialect, but where gentlemen spoke only our language. Arts, sciences, everything became French. German nationalism of the xix[th] century protested, shocked at this abjuration of Germany by herself. Her historians speak with shame of the long prevalence of French influence and civilization beyond the Rhine.

" The German patriot, " says Biedermann, " can only blush when looking back at the time when, while Louis XIV was annexing Empire States, with his haughty ambition, the blossom of the German nobility was rendering him its homage, feeling deeply honored if the last of his courtiers was good enough to approve so many exertions aiming at apeing the French Court. "

The Palatine princess[1] met in Paris seven princes, four counts, and other noblemen from her country. Later on the number of these courtiers still increased.

Who would believe to-day that the Germans of that time considered it an " honor to serve in the French army? " A remark made by a contemporary of the Great Frederick, Charles Ferdinand of Brunswick !

Under the orders of the King of France, thousands of them were making war for us against their own country. The famous name of the Marshall of Saxony[2] evokes the fusion reached by that Europe which a contemporary called : French Europe.

The experiments in internationalism we have witnessed nowadays and which ended in one of the most terrific struggles inflicted on the world, seem ridiculously artificial and petty when compared to such results. Impe-

1. Charlotte Elisabeth of Bavaria. Second wife of the Duke of Orleans, Louis XIV's brother.

2. Maurice, Count of Saxony (Son of August II Elector of Saxony and King of Polonia). Marshall of France. 1696–1750.

rial Germany, as she arose from her victories of 1870, has dreamed too, that, through the might of her arms, and the superiority of her "organization", she could impress on Europe a German stamp. France has used another way : although she could have disposed of strength, she employed persuasion. To Germany, after the horrors of the Thirty Years War, she has appeared like a saviour. Louis XIV carefully fostered what he called " his zeal for Germanic liberty, " and he knew how to distribute subsidies at the proper time to the princes, to the ministers, to the scientific and literary men of Germany

Speaking of Hevelius[1], Voltaire writes with irony : " Among the great men bred by that age, there's no one who testifies better than he, that this century can rightly be called that of Louis XIV. As Hevelius had lost an important library in a fire, the French monarch bestowed on the astronomer of Dantzig a gift representing much more than the loss. " It was a system continuing in

1. German Astronomer (1611-1687).

detail that of which the Westphalian Treaty formed the broad basis.

Biedermann, who, like a patriotic German of the new era, had studied, with wrath in his heart, the period of some hundred and fifty years when Germany was under France's domination, concludes that the advance made by the French, politically, explains the radiance of their civilization and genius. The so complete and firmly established State of Louis XIV disposed of every resource necessary to control, both in material and spiritual affairs, a Germany where the State was endowed with but rudimentary organs and had but a poor standard of life. In vain Leibniz [1] scolded the Germans for their fondness for foreign fashions, but he himself wrote his works in French, so much was he attracted by Louis XIV. For, this prince, says Biedermann, while dominating Germany, flattered her eminent man by the bestowal of all kinds of distinctions, thanks to the organization of great scientific Insti-

1. Illustrious German philosopher (1646-1716).

lutions, entirely lacking in Germany where these same men got no reward for their work. "Having no State worthy of the name, the German had lost the spring of any national and intellectual life. At that time, " organization " was on our side, supported by the allurements and the charm of our ideas and customs. Thus Labruyère [1] was entitled to compare Louis XIV with the " good shepherd, " who knows how to attach some by a golden chain, others by a voluntary subordination.

In the memoirs which he wrote for the Dauphin's instruction and which are the work of a mind broken to politics and willing that its experience should not be lost, Louis XIV has given prescriptions by which a State can take and keep a hold over its neighbours. He knew by what kind of springs men are moved. He knew that, if the disposal of strength is the condition of success, it is necessary to know how to temper its use. Why press the Germans when they are so

1. French moralist (1645-1696).

eager to serve ?   He shared the opinion of Gravel, one of his best agents in Germany, and who defined in the following terms the protectorate acquired by the King over the League of the Rhine :

'' This League gives an opportunity to your Majesty, to maintain the friends and the great credit you have in the Empire ; it opens the door to give indirect admission to Ministers approved by you in all its deliberations, and makes you practically a member of it, without binding you in any way ''.

In that sense Mignet[1] could say that Louis XIV was the real '' chief of the Empire ''...   And if the King, in the last period of his reign, ran the risk of stirring up what was so peaceful, and reopened a struggle which seemed closed to our advantage, it was not without the weightiest reasons.   The Affair of the Succession of Spain, awkwardly called '' the pivot of his reign '' by Mignet, who saw right but wrote wrong, continued the tradition of the great French policy.   The success of that endeavour opened a new era.

1. French historian (1796-1884).

Louis XIV had not resolved without hesitation to accept the will of Charles II, which called his grandson to the throne of Spain. At the grand Council of the crown, which was held on that occasion, the reason which prevailed was a State reason. France would achieve the scheme of François I, of Henri II, of Henri IV, of Richelieu; she would make an end, once and for all, of the " Spanish plan " and of any possibility of revival of such power as had been seen in Charles V's hands. Europe believed that Louis XIV dreamed of a universal monarchy, whereas strict balance was his only aim. To secure the separation of the Austrian dynasty from Spain, was a service to France and to the whole continent of Europe. By a wonderful turn of the tide, Europe, at last, rendered justice to Louis XIV, to his skill, to his foresight, when Emperor Joseph, having no heir at his death, in 1711, left as successor his brother Archduke Charles, the very one whom the coalition sustained against Philippe. The union of the two crowns, and the restoration of the Empire of Charles V appeared then as a danger much more threatening than the evil feared at first. Thanks to the political sense of the British conservatives, the Tories, when restored to power, a peace was concluded, which testified to the wisdom of Louis XIV.

The aim of the Spanish succession having been attained, the Habsburgs having been driven for ever off Madrid, and reduced to their hereditary estates, with the pompous but vacuous title of Emperors, Louis XIV had a thought which proves once more how far-reaching was that good-sense which Sainte-Beuve praised so highly.

At the end of his long career[1], a few months before his death, the old king had enjoyed the satisfaction of seing a cycle closed. That struggle against the Austrian dynasty which, through two centuries, had absorbed the monarchy, in which the whole French nation, with her kings, her great statesman, her illustrious captains, had taken part from the depth of her soul, that struggle

---

1. Grandson of Louis XIV, formerly Duke of Anjou. King of Spain from 1700-1746.

had come to an end. The question of Spain was solved to our advantage, as had been, sixty-seven years earlier, the question of Germany. France could rejoice. Her future on the continent was safe. She was at ease to perform the plan of her territorial unity, and of her expansion beyond the seas, a policy whose expression was to be found, later on, in the Family Pact[1] concluded with the Bourbons of Italy and Spain. Upon the intangible rule of the Westphalian Treaty, " necessary basis of the public peace, " Louis XIV conceived a new policy. The rivalry with the Austrian dynasty having no longer any object, he wanted to prevent the renewal of quarrels and wars henceforward useless for France. The fruits of a reconcilement between the two powers would be the consolidation of the results acquired. The Austrian dynasty, giving up her domination over Germany, would have an interest in preventing any other Germanic power from dominating over her in its turn. Weakened,

1. 1761.

diminished, therefore quieter and no more able to do harm. she passed to the rank of a conservative and moderating element. Although he remained ready to prevent and, eventually, to arrest by force of arms any revival of the ancient aims towards European supremacy so long cherished by Austria, Louis XIV saw in her a partner against the new tendencies already coming to light in some of the German countries He continued and developed Richelieu's system : after the Catholic German States, it was Austria he wanted to call into his alliance, in order to countervail the Protestant States, whose growth had been favored by circumstances.

The instructions given to the Count du Luc, in 1715, seven months before Louis XIV's death, furthered these views. The object of the Ambassador, — the first envoy, it is expressly mentioned, sent to Vienna in this quality, — shall be " to form, between the Houses of France and Austria, a union just as profitable to their respective interests, as necessary for the maintenance of general peace in Europe. "

The Count du Luc will have to represent to the Emperor that France no longer objects to the maintenance of the crown in his house and will even help him to prevent any other new power from taking it from him. Always on the alert, the royal diplomacy foresaw that, like the Habsburgs, forever diminished and worn out in Germany, having no longer any chance of establishing a great hereditary monarchy, the same ambition could accrue to some other powers which would lean towards the opposite element, that is to say, to the Protestants. It was a wonderful proof of sagacity and foresight to recognize that the great zeal of the Protestant princes for " Germanic liberty " would decrease as soon as one of them would discover any possibility of grasping that liberty for his own benefit. Two States were pointed out to the Count du Luc as being equally dangerous and as equally deserving to be kept in sight. One was the Electorate of Hanover, whose titulary had peculiarly increased in power since he had been called to the throne of England; the

other was the Kingdom of Prussia.   Hanover
and Prussia : the danger of a great German
Monarchy was again to appear from one of
these two quarters.   That very danger,
" the new union to be established between
the two dynasties of France and Austria, "
aimed precisely at checking it.

We must acknowledge that such perspica-
city and intuition for the future deserve the
warmest admiration.   Louis XIV, when he
died, left France well aware of a new peril.
He left, at the same time, the prescriptions
according to which the French could ward
it off.

*
* *

Politics consist in solving difficulties which
are renewed every day.   They consist, also, in
foreseeing these difficulties and in avoiding
any chance of being taken by surprise.
Thus, the expansion of Prussia gave the German problem a new aspect, and imposed new
concerns on French policy.

It would have been matter for wonder for
the contemporaries of Henri IV or of Riche-

lieu, if they had been told that the ancestor of the future Emperors of Germany was that very marquis of Brandenburg, a wretched sire ndeed, with nothing but sand-pits under his rule, and who, according to the fashion of so many German princes, lived under the shield of France for whose subsidies he was waiting as eagerly as might any beggar. Once promoted to the rank of Elector, the Marquis was yet far from being a considerable lord. Voltaire remarks that, at the Congresses of Westphalia, the Ambassadors of France had precedence over him and merely called him " Sir. " And Voltaire continues : " This very " Sir " was Frederick William, great-grand-father of the King of Prussia, Frederick. " A serious matter for wonder, indeed, is so rapid an ascension! The Hohenzollerns have grown at a speed no family has ever equalled. In a country like Germany where division was maintained by a system of balance in which first France, then Austria and the other secondary Courts after them, found their advantage in that parcelled Germany, how did one State, one alone, the Prussian State, succeed to swell, to rise above the other electoral or princely houses, to check two great powers, to represent the German Spirit, German patriotism, even, finally to realize, for its own benefit, that German unity against which a secular policy had multiplied its obstacles? It was not from themselves that the Hohenzollern estates could draw such a magnificent future. Neither Prussia, nor Brandenburg had any configuration of their own, any limits delineated by nature... No sign there, as in other countries, that there was room for a State, still less for a nation. The Kingdom of the Hohenzollerns could have been divided either a little further North, or a little further South. Its fate would have been the same, and alike, too, the task to be performed by that dynasty. Everything had to be done in these countries, poorly gifted by nature, and which came too late to occupy a position of importance in civilization. Everything, in fact, had to come out of man's hand, even the population, composed of refugees proceeding from all parts, and who, sooner or later, evicted the first inhabitants of Slavonic race : Prussia, that is Borussia, almost Russia.   She was treated by her masters like a colony, in the true sense of the word, a colony who lived and grew through her dynasty's labor.

Droysen[1], in the introduction to his *History of Prussian policy*, mentions that the Brandenburger Prussian State had its being neither upon the territory it involves, nor upon any common axis between the millions of subjects it gathered finally under its control. That state was always a " border State, " as Voltaire described it.   Yet again, according to Droysen, the history of Prussia shows in her growth such a continuity, in her orientation such a fixity, such an historical character as are to be found in similar degree only in the best constituted States, the richest in natural life.

That continuity, that fixity are precisely the fruits of an hereditary work : the Hohenzollerns have followed in the steps of the Capetians, the founders of the French Unity, of

1. German historian (1808-1884).

the Tsars " the assemblers of the Russian
soil. " But their work, from its outset,
has something cramped, artificial, which
again shows its amplified, monstrous proportions in the German Empire of nowadays.
" The union between the people and the
dynasty, " says Droysen, furthermore, " was
not the result of heredity, neither of election, nor of conquest, nor of any move
for the common defence or salvation after
a revolutionary storm... That union of
Prussia with her dynasty was realized by the
application of a political plan. " Indeed,
Prussia and Prussian greatness have been
worked out by the political conception of a
dynasty. Prussia's history is identified
with that of the Hohenzollerns. And it is
the history of a family which was unchan-
geable in its effort, and managed the
commonwealth under its rule as its did its
own estates. The Hohenzollerns behaved,
in the smallest details, like those peasants
who toil on their farm, enlarge it all around,
make money and rise, by dint of economy
and foresight. Before caring for the mission

of Prussia in Germany, and before aiming at an Empire, the Hohenzollerns have watched, as do the best heads of families, like careful and modest landlords, the husbanding and improving of their country. Before becoming electors, dukes, kings in Prussia, emperors in Germany, they climbed the first steps of fortune by the steady practice of rustic economy and by filling their cashbox.

Their start does not go back to the dark ages. They belong to a relatively recent time (xv[th] century). There is no legend in their connection. What is known shows that the common belief about the rise of monarchies is peculiarly erroneous. Neither to the splendor of their extraction, nor to their sword, nor even to their spirit of enterprise ought the Hohenzollerns to be grateful for their success. They refute the famous text :

" The first who became a king was but a lucky soldier! "

The founder of their house was merely lucky in his speculations : he was a little clerk in Nuremberg, fond of hoarding and a clever investor of money. Mirabeau, in his book on the *Prussian Monarchy*, was struck by this fact : " Frederick of Hohenzollern, he wrote, " had the good habit, a characteristic of his family, to keep a store in his safe. "

It is in this manner, so practical that it seems somewhat vulgar, but applied to a material always increasing and always acquiring larger proportions, that the Hohenzollerns succeeded in organizing the whole of Germany like a single enterprise which might include, to begin with, a barrack and a farm, then a mill. That one among them who, the first of his race, took the title of King, made use of the reserves in soldiers and florins stored up by the Great Elector, just as Frederick II was to use, later on, the Sergeant-King's savings.

If the Elector of Hanover made Louis XIV feel uneasy because he was King in England, the Elector of Brandenburg was suspicious to him because he had called himself King in Prussia. Exceptional circumstances were at work in order to enable the Hohenzollerns to attain the royal dignity : they had missed none of the opportunities at their hand. The great Elector had begun by freeing his Prussian dukedom from Polish control : he knew already how to deal with the poor Republic of Poland. Member of the Holy Empire, on account of his Electorate of Brandenburg, he was independent and his own master at home in Prussia. If, in the Holy Empire, there was no room for a King, that prohibition was not valid in Prussia, which was outside of the Empire. Frederick crowned himself there, in Kœnigsberg, on the 18th of January, 1701 : a great date in Prussian history. As his grandson was to write, later on, in the *Memoirs of Brandenburg* : " It was like a bait tendered by Frederick to his posterity, with more or less this meaning : I endowed you with a title. Now you must deserve it. I laid the ground for your greatness. Yours is now to complete the task. " From that very moment, according to John Stuart Mill's expression, Germany became a permanent possibility of annexation for Prussia. In fact, on the 178th anniversary of the crowning at Kœnigsberg, another Hohenzollern was proclaimed German Emperor at Versailles, in the Kings of France own palace.

Emperor Leopold had committed a blunder when he allowed Frederick to become a King in order to secure his alliance in the War of the Succession in Spain, an unsafe alliance, indeed, a help avariciously wrangled about, at any rate. It was an old custom for the Electors to swindle and rob the elected : the Brandenburger was consistent with the rule. Still, there had been neither lessons nor warnings lacking to prevent Leopold from the consequences of his mistake. If he found some counsellors — those whom Prince Eugene wanted to see hanged — who approved the crowning of a King in Prussia, others had objected that he was making room for a competitor, and endangering the future of the Austrian dynasty " exposed henceforth to lose the Empire through the rivalry of the House of Brandenburg whose power was constantly on the increase. " The more one studies history, the clearer it appears that very few are the cases where the great events were not perceived and understood in their germ by a small number of men, whom acquaintance with the laws of political physics enables to read the future. But far fewer are the cases when these men have received credit for their views.

Louis XIV, although he had done his best for the maintainance, with the Elector of Brandenburg, of such good relations as it was the rule in our diplomacy to foster with the German princes, was bitterly opposed to the rise of a Kingdom which, as he had supposed ought to become a centre of attraction for, Germany of the North and for Protestant Germany. Louis XIV foresaw the German unity achieved, no longer by Austria, but by Prussia, just as clearly as was possible in his time. Therefore, during twelve years, until the treaty of Utrecht, he refused to recognize the new Prussian Kingdom. It is very peculiar that the Holy See persisted in ignoring it for a longer time even than the King of France (till 1787). The Papacy,

which had disagreed with France, at the time
of the Westphalian treaties, formally censured
by the Church, had again met the French political point of view in regard of German affairs.
If it had depended upon Rome and France
alone, the two highest authorities of European civilization, the Prussian power would
have been still in its cradle, and the world
would not have known the Prussian scourge.
" We should fail by our duty, if we
could overlook such a fact, " wrote Clement XI[1] in his brief of April 16th, 1701.
Thus, by the Pope as by the King of France,
that is to say by the two chief elements of
order, Prussia was denounced as a public
danger for Europe. That dynasty, born
outside the Society of Nations in violation of
the principle of balance laid down, by
France's effort, in the 18th century, was
really revolutionary. Bound to push and
grow, like everything which lives, it could
do it only at the cost of the weightiest and
bloodiest of disorders. It could find its

---

1. Pope from 1700 to 1721.

way but by overthrowing all the ruling conventions, and from that very moment, war became fatally its " national industry." Let us mention the fact that the hideous future prepared by Prussia for Europe had been clearly discerned by the French monarchy and by the Papacy.

When the prince, who was to be called Frederick the Great, succeeded to his father, our representative in Berlin, the Marquis de Beauvau, sent to his Government a detailed report about the new King which is amazingly true to facts. The diplomatic corps in the old regime has always proved, as documents show, superiorly documented and sagacious. The Marquis de Beauvau told his Court that it would be imprudent to build too optimistic hopes upon Frederick II, according to what was known of him, while merely presumptive heir to the crown, and when his pranks, and his disputes with a severe father were Europe's gossip. Beauvau depicted Frederick such as he was to appear in reality : ambitious, calculating, given to concealment, " a dangerous neighbour, a suspi-

" cious and troublesome ally... " Enume-
rating the resources in money and men left
by the Sergeant-King to his son, the French
diplomat concluded : " Hence this power,
recently born in Europe, which in the
hands of the son becomes so formidable
that, in my opinion, it reverses the old
system or may, at least, change it. "
This was, summarized in a few words, the
whole contest which was about to divide
our country during the xviii[th] century.

The death of the Emperor Charles VI, — the
Ex-Archduke Charles, our late adversary in
the war for the succession in Spain, — seemed
again to open the Austrian question. Charles
left only a daughter, Maria-Theresa, to whom,
through an accumulation of treaties with all
the powers, and by collecting sealed documents, he supposed he had assured his inheritance. The Austrian sceptre being turned
into a distaff, was it not a good opportunity
for making an end, once and for all, of the
hereditary foe ? A great part of the public in
France was of that opinion. During two
centuries there had been a struggle against

the Habsburgs. The aim, now, was to crush them altogether to prevent any chance of their being elected again in the Empire, and, with that in view, to put in their place a friend of France, the Elector of Bavaria.

The Government, that of the prudent Cardinal Fleury[1], hesitated, weighing the pros and cons, without refusing support to the Bavarian, but satisfied that the house of Austria should remain as it was, still weakened with its control in the hands of a woman. The last and so wise advice of Louis XIV about the advantages of an understanding with the Court of Vienna, obviously came to all political minds. The safest seemed to wait, to see what might occur. This was Fleury's idea, and that, too, of Louis XV, still very young, still under a strict tutelage[2], but who did not lack in practical political sense. At the great Council where the attitude to be held by France was examined, Louis XV pronounced this peculiar view : " In my opi-

1. Minister of Louis XV (1653-1743).
2. The Regency, in the hands of Philippe, Duke of Orléans from 1715 to 1723.

" nion, we ought to retire upon Mount Pagnotte. " This was an old locution meaning such a position whence the fighting may be observed without taking part in it. Though timid, and somewhat lazy, Louis XV, whose perception was, through the effect of his education, of his rank also, and by virtue of the identity of his interest with the interest of the country, clear and perspicacious, was only wrong inasmuch as he did not know how to impose his will. Is there any surer proof that the more the monarchy prevails in a State, the better it is for the commonwealth, since, on this occasion, the king would have incurred no reproach, if he had shown a stronger hand.

The year 1741 marks in the history of our country a success for public opinion, the victory of a party over the royal policy, and that date has been fatal. A blind force, that of tradition, turned into a kind of routine, moved the masses who did not perceive that time had passed, and that the aspect of problems had changed. The danger began to rise in Berlin. The masses still saw it only in Vienna. The house of Austria was half dead, and yet, opinion wanted war, as in the past, with the house of Austria. The historian here meets a case of petrified instinct, similar to those noticed by the naturalists in the animal reign. Thus we see the wasps imitating the bees in vain and going on with the building of cells where they are unable to make honey. Likewise, obeying to some thoughtless impulse, French opinion, in which soldiers like the Marshall of Belle-Isle and the " philosophers " were in agreement, forced the Government's will in the affair of the Austrian succession[1].

However, the entrance of Prussia on the scene had a signification which imposed itself to the most heedless mind. The rape of Silesia really marked the beginning of a new era for Europe and in the relations of States. It is amusing to see, to-day, the heirs of the philosophy of the XVIIIth century protesting in the name of justice, against the invasion of Belgium, whilst the ancestors of William II, when they seized upon Silesia, received the

1. 1741-1748.

applause of the " philosophers " of the time. The theory of treaties considered as " scraps of paper, " before being condemned, when professed by Bismarck or Bethmann-Hollweg, did not horrify either Voltaire or d'Alembert, or any of the partisans of " natural right " provided that the theory was exposed and practised by Frederick II, idol of the liberal minds. But how was this possible? The right violated by Frederick was not a right of nature. It was the Statute of the Society of Nations ; it was the law on which the European world lived ; it was a progress obtained by might at the service of reason ; it was the assembly of conventions which, such as they were, made Europe nearly habitable, assured to France a privileged place, spared her people the scourge of invasion and its corollary, the scourge of an armed peace. The apparition of the Prussian policy announced the most terrible evils to Europe and civilization, and threatened them with a return to barbarity. 1740, 1870, 1914 will certainly appear to all future historians, in their connexity, with their fatal and mysterious tie. Our kings, our diplomats had understood that relation. It is humiliating for the public opinion of the people which calls itself the most quick-witted in the world that it did not have even the slightest presentiment of it.

The protest of Maria-Theresa [1] against the rape of Silesia was, however, most eloquent. It remarkably resembled that of the King of the Belgians calling for help against William II. The Queen appealed to all the powers, and firstly, to the one which guaranteed the European equilibrium, to oppose the Prussian robbery. " An Austrian envoy, " said the Queen, " was still at Berlin when, favored by this same pacific appearance, the King of Prussia has invaded a foreign land and troubled the repose of a friendly province. One can judge from that with what fate all princes are theatened, if such conduct is not punished by them by a mutual effort. This does not refer, therefore, to Austria alone, but to the whole Empire and *to the*

1. 1717-1780. Daughter of the Emperor Charles VI. Empress of Germany. Queen of Hungary and Bohemia. Married Francis of Lorraine.

whole of Europe. It is the business of all Christian princes not to allow the most sacred ties of human society to be broken with impunity. All must join the Queen and furnish her with the means of preserving them from such a danger. As to herself, she will oppose fearlessly *to the common enemy* all the forces which God has given her, and, for this service rendered to the general welfare, she will not ask for any other reward than the reparation of the prejudices which her States have suffered and whatever will be necessary to guarantee them against such assaults in the future. " This language we shall hear again. It was not only Europe which was interested in breaking the Prussian policy. Already, it was the whole world. The rape of Silesia had the same consequences as the aggression against Belgium. Blood was shed in parts of the planet most remote from Prussia. This is what Macaulay has demonstrated, with eloquence, in a famous page :

" Had the Silesian question been merely a question between Frederick and Maria-Theresa, it would be impossible to acquit the Prussian

King of gross perfidy. But when we consider the effects which his policy produced aud could not fail to produce on the whole community of civilized nations, we are compelled to pronounce a condemnation still more severe. On the head of Frederick is all the blood which was shed in a war which raged during many years and in every quarter of the globe, the blood of the column of Fontenay, the blood of the mountaineers who were slaughtered at Culloden. The evils produced by his wickedness were felt in lands where the name of Prussia was unknown; and in order that he might rob a neighbour whom he had promised to defend, black men fought on the coast of Coromandel and red men scalped each other by the great Lakes of North America. "

Likewise, we shall have seen, in 1914, the Japanese entering, lined up, on Chinese territory, and black tribes slaughtering each other in the heart of Africa.

The bad results of the first Seven Years' War [1]

1. 1741-1748.

did not fail to strike political minds.   It was
evident that France had taken the wrong road,
worked against herself for the greatness of
Prussia and, literally, for the King of Prussia.
Frederick had played with the French alliance.
He had miserably betrayed us by approaching
England.   His young power was growing and
showed that it had long teeth already.   Moreover, the ascendency taken by Frederick was
becoming dangerous.   He appeared as a
possible federator of the Germanies, while the
Austrian dynasty had just proved again that
her vitality was decreasing and that she could
no more aspire to supremacy over the German
countries.

Already, however, the Oriental problem
was laid before her ; new interests were divert-
ing her from Germany, and displacing her
centre of gravity.   It is under these conditions, and after the sad experience of the
Prussian friendship, that the idea of the
famous " reversal of the Alliances, " — such
as Louis XIV, in his instructions to the
Count du Luc, and later on, the Marquis de
Beauvau, in his report from Berlin, had consi-

dered timely, — ripened in the mind of Louis XV's government.

* *

The contemporary historical school has done away with a certain number of legends propagated by the historians of the romantic school.   Albert Sorel, in particular, has established what Michelet[1] had bitterly denied : namely, that the system, inaugurated in 1756, of an alliance with Austria, was the fruit of a long thought-out political conception. When a newspaperman or an orator, developing some censure upon the old regime, quotes Louis XV and the reversal of the alliances, he immediately reveals the amount of his knowledge.   The same man, however, will not fail, in other circumstances, to praise Sorel's work, for there is no sure relation between the celebrity of an author and the diffusion of his ideas.

Man is so made that he gives up only with

1. French historian (1798-1874).

reluctance a polemical argument which he has easily at hand and which he knows will always be echoed by the public. If the mysterious word of " reversal of the Alliances " is, in half-cultivated minds, mingled to the idea of " the faults of the Monarchy, " it is through the prolongation of very old impressions, of vague reminiscences, through the hereditary suggestion of disputes raging among the French for a hundred and fifty years. The study of the movements of public opinion during the xviii^{th} century demonstrates, strikingly, that the disagreement which emerged in about 1740, and matured in 1756, — the proper direction to give to French foreign policy, has been the exact origin of the separation which was to break out a few years later between the people and the Bourbons. For long disputes raged about the fundamental cause of this divorce between a dynasty and a nation which, during eight centuries, had been intimately united to such an extent that it was always in the popular element that the Capetians had found their support, whereas the gravest difficulties

had come to them from the influential nobility.   It is from the reversal of the alliances "
that most certainly dates the origin of the
Revolution which was to go as far as regicide,
after having begun with the simple desire for
reforms in legislation, rural economy and
administration.   It was about a question of
national interest where, as a succession of
events had proved, the monarchy was in the
right, that a misunderstanding arose, bound
to embitter up to the rupture.

As long as the publication of authentic
documents had not brought things to light,
the reversal of the Alliances had its legend.
For some time, it was considered as certain
that every kind of foresight and of political
calculation had been wanting in this change of
front, in this reconciliation with the court of
Vienna.   Alone caprice and vanity had a part
in that evolution.   A favorite [1], and a court
abbot had been the toys of the Austrian diplomacy.   Bernis [2] would have stepped into the

1. Antoinette Poisson, Marquise de Pompadour (1721-
1764).

2. Cardinal de Bernis (1715-1794).

Marquise de Pompadour's intrigue flattered to be called " dear friend " in a letter from the Empress (a legend denounced by history and accredited by Frederick II himself). A boudoir diplomacy would have thrown France into this adventure, compromised our interests, altered our political system, handed over our old allies, our real friends (the Prussians) to the discretion of Austria. Still more, this treason would have been accomplished in the name of the detestable solidarity of the clerical and reactionary powers. The fanaticisms would have leagued themselves against Frederick, Champion of the Reform, and, consequently, of liberalism and light.

The xv[th] volume of Michelet's *History of France* develops this theme with gusto. What curious reading is this book to-day when the liberal point of view is reversed! The Hohenzollerns and Prussian militarism are exalted, by Michelet, as being the real builders of modern times. Michelet does not only praise the " great king of Prussia, " " truly great. " He extols (how ironically these words sound at the present moment) the " boundless, moral consequences of his reign. " Frederick has been the creator of Germany, the Siegfried who awakened this Brunhilda ; and idealistic, virtuous Germany, whose renaissance as a nation was to be one of the instruments of progress, a promise of regeneration for humanity, was the fetish of Michelet.   It is not the panegyric of the King of Prussia alone, but of the Germanic genius of which he is the superior incarnation.   " The Austrians themselves, while deploring to make war against him, felt the German in the Prussian.   One man's admiration re-opened the generous source of fraternity. The cult of the hero gave them back their Germania. "   Without any doubt, Frederick was a conqueror who placed brutal force at his service.   But, " one observes in him a beautiful accomplishment; his feats of war-fare, he sees them from high. "   Vainly it was attempted to blacken the memory of Frederick, to turn his cynicism against him.   In reality, " he has but one stain : his association in the partition of Poland. "   And yet, the

Jesuits, in Michelet's eyes, are his true inspirers.

In opposition to this hero of Germanic loyalty, what does Michelet show us at work at the Court of Vienna? That, also, is very curious, when re-read in 1915 to the sound of the maledictions covering Prussian perfidy. For Michelet, for history such as it had been written up to 1870, it was the Slavonic sycophants who had joined with Tartuffe [1] against the loyal Hohenzollern. Kaunitz, Maria-Theresa's Minister, the author of the Franco-Austro-Russian coalition which very nearly crushed Prussia, Kaunitz receives this outrage, — supreme during Michelet's time — : " He is a Slav, an hypocritical Slav, a Slav with a German mask! "... What a contrast with a loyal German like Frederick !

Michelet's historical romance is a scandal for the intellect when confronted with the results which the greatness of Prussia has meant for France, for Europe and for civilisation... It is the opprobrium of science and of criticism when compared to the careful

1. Tartuffe ; a character personifinig bigotted hypocrisy, in a play by Molière.

deliberations, to the examination of the inconveniences and advantages of the affair, examination which preceded the reversal of the alliances. With complete lucidity, recalling the successive and unhappy experiences which he had just made with the King of Prussia, the royal Government decided to adopt a new system. And that, of course, not in order to change the policy of France in regard of Germany, still based on the treaties of Westphalia ("which assured France, so long as she follows the proper way, the control over Germany," said Bernis), but to adjust this policy to new circumstances and requirements.

Albert Sorel was right when he said that this idea had not been born in a day nor in a few minds. A thorough preparation had matured it. How far we are from rashness and whim! In 1737, in 1749, in 1750, in 1752, the instructions given to our Ambassadors in Austria disclose the assiduous reflections of the Government. In 1750, the instructions of the Marquis d'Hautefort distinctly say : "The King is not in the least affected by the ancient suspicions which, since the reign of

Charles V, have caused the house of Austria to be regarded as a dangerous rival of the house of France. The enmity between these two great powers must no longer be a State reason." The instructions which Bernis elaborated seven years later for the ambassador of the King at Vienna, exposed all the motives for which the King resolved to take that final step and to approach the Court of Vienna. It is a memorandum of great seriousness and depth of conception, without a single weakness. The man chosen to fulfill this mission was, besides, one of the most capable in his days : he was none other than Choiseul[1]. The main points of the directions that he took with him, were :

" By uniting himself to the Court of Vienna, it can be said that the King has changed the political system of Europe. But, it would be wrong to think that he altered the political system of France. The political object of this crown has been, and always will be, to fill the superior part

1. Étienne-François, Duc de Choiseul. Minister of Foreign Affairs under Louis XV (1719-1785).

becoming its age, dignity and majesty in the European community; to resist any power which would attempt to overrule it, be it by trying to usurp its possessions, be it by claiming an unjust preeminence, be it, in a word, by undermining its influence and credit in the general affairs. "

Follows an historic survey of the conflicts of the house of France with the house of Austria since Charles V. " Until 1755, the King has been inspired by the maxims of his predecessors. " On all sides, in Germany, Spain, Italy, the Habsburgs have been beaten and repelled. France has grown up upon their ruins. Louis XV has again enlarged the Kingdom with the Duchy of Lorraine and Bar; Alsace and French Flanders are secure owing to the destruction of Friburg and of the principal fortresses of Austrian Flanders. But, what has happened in these later times? Here the instructions become luminous and nearly prophetic. One would believe they had been composed to deter Napoleon III from working for the welfare of Piedmont and of Prussia.

" To effectuate such great things, the King made use of the King of Sardinia, in 1733, and of the King of Russia in 1741, as Cardinal Richelieu had formerly used the crown of Sweden and of several princes of the Empire, with this difference, however, that the Swedes, poorly paid by France, have remained faithful to her and that, by empowering the Kings of Sardinia and of Prussia, we have but made these two princes ingrates and rivals, great and important lesson which must warn us, once and for all, to govern one and the other monarch rather by fear and hope, than by extension of territory[1]. We must also win over the princes of the Empire to our system more by protection than

1. It is interesting to observe that, on this point, Cardinal de Bernis meets Montesquieu. In his unpublished *Mélanges* issued in our day, one sees that Montesquieu, in 1748, was alarmed at the growth of Prussia and judged it madness to favor it any longer. Referring to Sardinia, he was not less categorical. " One lift more, " said he of the Duke of Savoy, " and we will make him master of Italy and he will be our equal. " What Montesquieu had not foreseen is this : that he was himself destined to help a Great Prussia and a great Italy by opening the gate, with his political philosophy, to the revolutions and constitutions that had to leave France of the xviii[th] century so unarmed against her rivals.

by subsidies; in general, the one and the others should depend upon us for their needs, but it will always be very dangerous to make our system depend on their gratitude. ''

The King of Prussia had betrayed our confidence; neither was it safe to rely upon the thankfulness or fidelity of Austria, but on the common interest of both States. Choiseul was told to '' seize the mean between blind faith and unjust suspicion. '' Finally, the instructions concluded whit some wise words. '' The new alliance is like all human works. It has its faults. '' It '' embraces too many objects not to present some danger ''. Therefore, its development must be watched without, however, being hampered by the idea of its inconveniencies and perils. '' All must be foreseen, but not all feared. '' Thus, the Austrian alliance was reduced to the just proportions of an affair which opportunity commanded and where France was to find her profit.

It is a very strange phenomenon that a diplomatic operation, conceived and executed by such cool and calculating minds, should have assumed, in the popular imagination, the character of a plot between the dark powers of fanaticism, of corruption and of immorality. Several causes have contributed to this. The first is that the multitude does not like new ideas. It prefers the beaten tracks. It adheres to tradition, the one which imposes itself by force of habit, at random, no matter whether this tradition be beneficial or not, or whether it has ceased to be either. The French monarchy, by adapting its system of foreign policy to new conditions, provedt self to be skilfully supple and innovating. The mass of the nation did not follow it, but remained lazily in the rut, chained to a dead past. Perhaps it would have ended by understanding and by following the Government if the leaders of public opinion, (they were " philosophers "), had been capable of enlightening it. But these were pledged to the same error by their ideas, by their self-love and by the party they had adopted.

Was it chance or calculation? It happened that the Hohenzollern whose policy aimed at

the destruction of the European system established by the xvii[th] century, declared himself
a friend and protector of the adepts of ideas
which themselves aimed at the overthrow of
the existing order of things. The ambition
of the Kings of Prussia could not be satisfied
with less than a complete change of scenery
in Europe. The alliance of their policy with
the philosophical movement out of which the
Revolution was to spring is thus explained.
As soon as a sharp calculator like Frederick
had understood the advantages which the
sympathies of French liberalism granted him,
he cultivated them assiduously by advances
and flatteries in which the well-coined arguments did not fail to reinforce the doctrine.
Besides, their being Protestants, an important
title in the eyes of the adversaries of the
Church, the Hohenzollerns thus became the
champions of European liberalism. It is
more than a bitter irony, it is the scandal of
our history that Prussian militarism and
absolutism should have been flattered in
France, during one hundred and fifty years,
as the organ and expression of liberty and of

" modern ideas, " before being denounced to the horror and execration of the civilized word in the name of the same ideas.

This mad cult of Prussia still increased when the somewhat dry principles of the Encyclopædia had been enriched by Rousseau's sentimentality. The axiom of natural right represented the political structures, the modest shelters of diplomacy, as monstrous impediments to the supreme goodness of man such as he comes into the world, still pure from all the corruptions of Society. It was the treaties, the combinations, the inventions of the Kings and of the nobility which kept the conflicts burning, and bred the hated wars ; thus spoke the " Contrat Social " and Rousseau's doctrine of which Voltaire said it made you long to walk on all fours. Only leave the people alone ; races shall form themselves into nations of their own free will within the limits fixed by nature, and humanity will at last enjoy peace.

Frederick, who had gained ground by the vogue of the Encyclopædia as a champion of light, gained ground also by the vogue of the

" Contrat Social, " as champion of Germanism. Contemporaries, even disciples of Rousseau, Raynal, Mably, whose books were immensely popular (Napoleon read them), spread the principle which was to become famous under the name of " principle of the nationalities. " Henceforth in France and out of France, the cause of liberalism and of the Revolution, on the one hand, and the cause of the Hohenzollerns on the other, were bound together. And thus the philosophers flattered the misoneist passions and the simplicity of the multitude. They seemed the " liberal forerunners, " they represented progress in opposition to the reactionary forces (Bourbons, Habsburgs), while, by serving the cause of Prussia as they did, their childish and summary mode of thought prepared a return to barbarity and procured to civilisation, for generations to come, the darkest destinies.

The fact that the writers who were the champions of freedom, in the xviii[th] century, in spite of their pretensions to be " the lights, " have not seen, have indeed refused to see the Prussian peril, is crushing for their political philosophy. Not only were such spirits apt to expose France to the worst catastrophies the day they would govern her, but their error itself proved their incapacity to understand the march of events and to serve the very progress that they claimed to personify. By facing Prussia, and approaching Austria, the French Monarchy had established that one had to " rise above a prejudice three centuries old. " The philosophers had neither the vigor, nor the intellectual liberty necessary to reject the weight of this prejudice. They have revealed the servility of their mode of thought, and their attachment to routine. They put themselves on the same level as the ignorant and credulous crowd. And it is this crowd which had to pay later on for this sin against the spirit. The French of the xviii[th] century who despised the work of our Kings and of their Ministers, who rebuilt the world on " clouds, " did not sufficiently appreciate the advantages of their age. They knew nothing about obligatory and universal conscription. They did not know what invasion was. From all points of view, letters, art, or commerce, they have been benefited, in " French Europe ", through the political prestige, and the ascendency conquered by the labor of royalty. And it was they who complained! We should like to see them in the Europe of iron and blood which they have bequeathed to us.

* *

The coalition of France, Austria and Russia, the fear of which was later to give Bismarck night-mares, was so well conceived that it nearly caused the complete destruction of the Prussian power. Had it not been for the Empress Elisabeth's death, which changed the course of Russian policy, Frederick II would have succumbed. By the peace he signed, in 1763, at Hubertsburg, he showed that he had failed to attain the place he coveted in the Empire. But he kept Silesia, while we kept all our continental positions : thus, from this point of view, the second Seven Years War[1] had had no result, procured no material

1. 1756-1763.

advantage to France.   It is only in our time that it was realized that, by stopping the progress of Frederick II in Germany, by retarding the Hohenzollerns in their ascension towards the Empire, this war had not been completely sterile.

But, it had been thoroughly unpopular. While France was fighting against the King of Prussia, public opinion was Prussophile. At Paris, wishes favorable to Frederick were expressed aloud and his successes were warmly cheered.   In the army itself, many an officer, from hate for the Austrian ally, did not hide his sympathies for the adversary.   Such was the case of a future Minister of the Revolution, Dumouriez.   And then, the naval war with England, which had developed simultaneously with the continental war, had ended in a disaster.   Public opinion, in reality, did not care much for the colonies, if we remember Voltaire's famous saying about '' the acres of snow in Canada! '' Still, the treaty of Paris was bitterly resented.   The responsibility was made to fall on the Austrian policy.   The new alliance was, cause of all the evil, and those who had signed it were guilty of treason. This idea, which was so new, that the King, the heir of those who had made France, with whom France had, until then, formed but one body and one soul, could be suspected of treason, that idea rose for the first time in the public mind. The scaffold of Louis XVI, and of the " Autrichienne ", could, henceforth, appear to others besides to the thaumaturgus Cagliostro[1].

Owing to this misunderstanding which was bound to increase with time, the task of the Government became singularly hard. The complications, the mysteries with which the foreign policy of Louis XV was surrounded in the last part of his reign, were due to the difficulty which the King had met, when manœuvring in broad day-light. Thenceforward, not only in public opinion, but in the Ministries, and even in the near vicinity of the throne, there will be a party, the Prussophile party, which blames, mocks,

1. Joseph Balsamo, Count of Cagliostro. Famous quack, physician and occultist, born in Sicilia (1743-1795).

refuses its adhesion, raggles over its coopera-
tion, and even, perhaps (the good intention,
the certainty that one has truth on one's side
justifying all), will not see any harm in
revealing the Government's plans to the good
friend at Berlin.   Thus, the King finds himself driven to his famous " secrecy " : this is
the conclusion which meets the historian who
studies its directions and mechanism without
bias.

But, open or secret, the policy of the monarchy is for ever stamped with suspicion.
Whatever it attempts, it will never efface the
impression left by the " reversal of the
alliances, " and the year 1756 remains the
critical date of our national history.   The
foreign policy of Louis XVI and of Vergennes is the most honest, the most reasonable, the most farseeing, the most national
which can be imagined.   At the outset, there
were exaggerations in the Austrian sense : it
corrects them.   By sea, it takes a striking
revenge on England, and recuperates a part of
our colonies.   In Europe, all the elements
capable of upsetting the equilibrium are closely

watched. Never has French diplomacy reached such a high and clear conception of the part which the Treaties of Westphalia had granted to our country. Besides, an attentive control was more than ever necessary. The Continental problems had been complicated, in the middle of the xviii[th] century, by colonial competitions[1]. Under Louis XVI, it is by their relation with the Oriental question that the difficulties have to be solved : Vergennes has this great intuition and establishes the foundations of the method to be followed. But nothing can be done, the charm is broken. France does not understand.

Had it not been for that great folly, the Revolution, France's path was clearly traced out for her : it is what a mind such as Renan's has perceived at certain hours, with the consciousness of the error committed.

1. In this connection, it is very curious that, when saying that Canada and India were lost by Louis XV, one never speaks of America as lost by the English parliamentary regime, in consequence of the assistance Louis XVI lent to the American Revolution. It was, however, beautiful reparation for the Treaty of Paris, and within exactly twenty years (1763-1783).

In Germany, especially, it sufficed to impose respect for the equilibrium and to utilize that right of " Guarantee " which the Treaty of 1648 reserved to the Crown of France and which was neither so " insufficiently defined, " nor so " inefficacious " as has been said, since, in 1779, at Teschen, the intervention of our country completely checked an offensive return of Frederick II against Germany. On the verge of the Revolution, the masterly instructions given to the Baron de Breteuil, our Ambassador at Vienna, those to the Count d'Esterno, plenipotentiary at Berlin, testify to the sagacity and firmness of the views which the French Monarchy extended to German affairs. The Austrian alliance is kept in a conditional and relative place. What is and what remains absolutely certain is the principle that no one is to have the upper hand in Germany and that the King of France remains the protector of Germanic liberties.

It is upon this immutable basis that the Austrian Alliance was concluded. For, it can no more be allowed to Austria, though an ally, than to Prussia, to do anything which would tend to abolish or shake the principles laid down by the Westphalian Treaty. This Treaty is permanent as is also France's guarantee, " one of the most efficacious means that she could employ to check the ambition and restlessness of the great powers of Germany. " This ambition, this " restlessness, " in other words the German delirium, the *furor teutonicus*, — knew no obstacles from the very day when, through the Revolution, the barriers of the Treaties of Westphalia were upset.

It was the work of several centuries which was going to be frustrated. It was a new period, a period of regression which was opening for France and for the European commonwealth.

CHAPTER IV

THE REVOLUTION AND THE EMPIRE PREPARE
THE UNITY OF GERMANY

By dint of considering the Revolution sometimes as the supreme principle of good, sometimes as the supreme principle of evil, sometimes as a complete regeneration of society, as the opening of a new era in the history of mankind, and sometimes, on the contrary, as a work of hell, one has ended in spreading the illusion that the date of 1789 had, by virtue of some magic wand, marked a radical separation between two epochs. The habit has been acquired of believing that, between the ancient regimen, and the revolutionary regimen, there had been no connexion, that an unexpected event had suddenly called to

life ideas, situations and men until then
entirely unknown. This childish conception,
which for long prevailed in France, has rendered unintelligible the larger part of the
circumstances of the Revolution itself, and the
course which this Revolution followed.

History knows no miracles. Logic in
continuity is her chief law. By its complexity, by the mass of elements it puts
in movement, politics are like nature : they do
not proceed by leaps. The taking of the Bastille, which later appeared as a symbol and
had only been effected by a gang of rioters
unknown to the rest of Paris, had neither
prevented the King himself, Louis XVI [1], from
hunting as usual, nor the Parisians from going
to the theatre, that very same day. Neither had
it prevented other events from following their
course in the rest of the world, nor made a
clear table of Europe. When Revolution in
itself is considered, neither as a Messianic
apparition, nor as an Apocalyptical monster,

1. Grandson of Louis XV, 1754-1793. Married Marie-
Antoinette, Archduchess of Austria, daughter of Marie-
Thérèse, Empress of Germany.

but in its relations with the interests, the tendencies, the impulsions, the customs, the
positions taken and the course of European
affairs in the midst of which it supervened,
the event is reduced to its just proportions and
the consequences become explained. If not
viewed in this light it seems but a furious and
confused fray, of which the mind looses the
clue.   It then becomes easier to judge of its
convulsions, simply from the apologetical and
moral standpoint.   Hence, between Frenchmen, a new subject of division and quarrels,
which disappears of itself as soon as are
understood the different causes whose concordance has so far impelled the actors of the
Revolution.

At the moment when Louis XVI convoked
the General States, there were many questions
pending in Europe.   The most foolish illusion consists in imagining that the European
world held its breath while contemplating the
wonders which were taking place in Paris.
The affairs in the East, the affairs of Poland,
the affairs of the Netherlands were the concern
of the governments.   They perceived at once

the events of France as a new factor which had dropped into their policy and they were not affected by it otherwise. For, neither revolutions, nor the fall of monarchies were new things in Europe and the foreigner had no reason for wondering that France should start on the path were England, the Netherlands, Portugal, Sweden, Poland, America, etc., had preceded her. As a rule, revolutions were phenomena regarded so calmly that the monarchies assisted them sometimes when they did not actually foment them. Louis XIV tendered the recipe to the Dauphin when he taught him how he had himself supported the remainder of Cromwell's faction, granted subventions to the republicans of Holland, and excited the Hungarians against the Emperor. Louis XVI, in his turn, had come to the rescue of the American insurgents, and England, — the fact is well-known to-day, — did not miss the opportunity, in 1789, of paying him back in his own coin.

Among foreign governments, some accepted the events of France with equanimity, others with such satisfaction that, according to

Mr. Waddington's expression, the " King of Prussia was very near making vows for the perpetuation of the revolutionary troubles. "

One reads again, in the *Manuel de politique étrangère* by M. Émile Bourgeois, who, on many points, condenses the conclusions of the present-day school of history : " The political men of the xviii[th] century were not guided by reasons of sentiment. Towards the French revolution they felt neither benevolence, nor real hostility. They judged it as a fact, and according to the opinion formed in their circle and among their predecessors upon facts of the same kind. They remembered that England's civil discords had, during the whole of the xvii[th] century, kept her apart from European affairs and that Holland had been enslaved to her neighbours as a result of the struggle between the Stahouders and the States. " At the news of the events in Paris, the idea which occurred obviously to all those who governed Europe, was that the embarrassments of the King of France were welcome. This one reckoned that he would have a free hand in Germany, this other in Poland, the third on the seas. And each of them took measures to adjust his own policy to the interior crisis of France.

But, on the other hand, in France herself, life continued as usual. No more at that time than at any other did one see entirely new men taking prominent positions. Thiers[1] has remarked, when relating the vicissitudes of the monarchical restoration in 1814, that these events had unfurled themselves on the same background as the Terror, the Directory, the Consulate and the Empire. By the natural effect of the slowness with which generations succeed to each other, by the insensible gradation of the ages, one sees at all epochs old men and mature men collaborating with younger ones, and through the influence of business experience and of acquired authority, the ideas and sentiments of the anterior period yet impose themselves, after the institutions and the customs seem to have undergone a complete transformation. In order to understand the policy of the Revolu-

1. French statesman and historian. 1797-1877. President of the French Republic (1871).

tion, the greatest account must be taken of the fact that the men to whom she owed her initial direction and the rudderstroke which was going to mark out her way for twenty-five years, brought forth ideas and prejudices formed under the former regimen. These men were directly under the influence of the opinion which had reigned a generation earlier. They represented the discontent which had spread at the end of the reign of Louis XV, and it was to that discontent that they had a natural tendency to obey. Of the two men who, in 1792, drew the Revolution and France into such a fatal path, the one, Dumouriez[1], was at that date, fifty-three, the other, Brissot[2], twenty-eight years old. Both were born to the intellectual world at the moment when, as we have just observed, the French people had begun to disagree with the monarchy on the subject of the alliances. With the rest of the great

1. Dumouriez (Charles-François), 1739-1824; French general; won the Battles of Valmy et Jemmapes.

2. Brissot (Jacques-Pierre), 1754-1793; member of the Convention.

public, they had been nurtured on the anti-Austrian and Prussophile passion. Once in possession of power, it is this very passion, the great passion of their ardent time, the time when all ideas crystallize in the later part of life, that they had at heart to gratify.

It is in this sense that we must understand the " principle of continuity " which Albert Sorel referred to in the great historical work which made his reputation, when asserting that it was the law and the leading principle of the French Revolution. For in truth, the Revolution, in her European work, did not continue the ancient *régime* at all; yet she pretended to continue it, and even with improvements. Through the most curious phenomenon, she affected to go back to the pure traditions of French policy, as if these traditions had been discarded by the two last kings since the reversal of the alliances. In this sense, the Revolution has been truly reactionary. To what extent the date of 1756 controls her course, appears clearly in the famous text where the *Comité de salut public* declared : " From Henri IV until 1756, the

Bourbons have not committed one single capital mistake. " It was in 1756, through the treaty of Versailles, and the alliance with the house of Austria, that the " capital mistake " had been committed. This very mistake the triumphant Revolution assumed to repair.

It is necessary to remember that, in 1792, France was just as officially the ally of Austria, as she is to-day the ally of Russia. But this alliance was unpopular. It was attacked on all sides and all the forces of feeling had been associated against her. Of course, political reasons were not lacking for the justification of sentimental repugnances. In order to open war against Austria, the Girondins made use of arguments presented by professional men. Favier's writings determined the leading doctrine and, under Louis XV, Favier had belonged to diplomacy and had even been an agent employed by the " King's secrecy. " A certain knowledge of European affairs and skilful management of diplomatic language endowed Favier with a sort of authority, when he censured " the aberration of our political system of 1756, " when he granted that, whatever had been the defections and disloyalties of Frederick, yet a common interest joined France and Prussia against the Habsburgs. It is the argument of Favier which Michelet reproduces, purely and simply, in his *History*, when he writes, after relating the reversal of the alliances: " Now, Austria will have Germany in her power. " Where the true aberration was, has been too clearly shown by events, since Germany, after having, for so long, belonged to nobody, ended, as a result of the blunders of the Revolution, in falling under Prussia's yoke.

*
*   *

The contemporary historical school which rose, under Sorel's lead, to an irreproachable impartiality, allowed nothing to subsist of the legend according to which the European Kings would have leagued together against the Revolution in order to give their crown back to the Bourbons. The coalition had, not without irony, invoked the pretext of legitimity, while taking absolutely no interest in

the fate of Louis XVI and of Marie-Antoinette : it is well known that the Convention,
in spite of several attempts, did not succeed
in its plan of exchanging the Queen. The
truth is that the coalition used so weakly,
however, when not absurdly, the contra-
revolutionary argument, that the Republicans,
although having declared war against the
tyrants, were not long before negotiating
with them. The rule of the Kings in their
contact with the Revolution was that of a
" sacred selfishness. " This was the thought
expressed by the Emperor Leopold, Marie-
Antoinette's brother, when he wrote, with
perfect calm : " Our aim is not at all to make
war on France, to lavish our gold and our
blood in order simply to replace her in her
former state of power. "

The truth is, also, that the Revolution was
eager for war and provoked it. It was deliberately that the legislative Assembly declared
war on Austria. Jean Jaurès in his *Histoire
socialiste* insisted upon the responsibility of
Brissot and of the Girondins and covered
them with his malediction for having deterred

the Revolution from her normal course and plunged Europe into a series of conflagrations for twenty-three years.   But, could the Revolution have been pacific?   Could it even last, if it had preserved peace?   Mirabeau anticipated the future; he understood the implacable logic of events, when he implored the Constituante to arm France : " Look at the free nations, " said he prophetically, " it is by more ambitions, more barbarous wars that they have always marked their way... Do you not suppose that popular excitement, if ever you deliberate here about war, will not some day bring about disastrous conflicts ? " This movement had to burst forth the very day some orators were to make an appeal to the passions of popular opinion the day when the new institutions, having handed over foreign policy, as well as the rest, to the intrigues and plots of partisanship, to the designs of the ambitious, to the fancies of the Assemblies and of the mob, the question of the relations with the foreign world would no more be settled according to the interests of France, but to sentiments and theories simple enough to flatter both the spirit of system and the instincts of democracy.

The year 1792, up to the declaration of war of the 20th of April, was filled with the desperate resistances which the monarchy, remaining faithful to its *rôle* of guardian of the national interest, opposed to the war-like will of the Assembly and of opinion : last phase of a pathetic struggle between blindness and wisdom. Although represented by a somewhat common-place King, royalty was, nevertheless, according to Renan's[1] expression, the brain of the nation, while there could not be a greater confusion of errors, illusions and false calculations than those committed by the Assembly. The more so since it was intoxicated by the enthusiastic approval of the mob in the tribunes. About the dispositions of Prussia and of England, about the resources of the Emperor, about the military preparation of France, Brissot and his friends erred lamentably; they gratified themselves with empty words, which received the warmest applause.

1. Ernest Renan. Great French writer, 1823-1892.

Strange inversion of the *rôles* which one hundred years of Revolutionary pleas wrongfully attributed to the two contrary elements, the rising democracy and the sinking royalty. Wisdom, examining spirit, and experimental method are on the side of the Bourbons, and of a few aristocrats by birth or genius (Mallet du Pan, Rivarol, etc.), who still surround them, and who, being more or less partisans of the new ideas, have kept a clear notion of the public interest. On the opposite side, fanaticism, the flattest routine, the tyranny of learned sentences are the lot of these brilliant orators, of this mob furiously bent on its own ruins.

1792 essentially marks a regression of fifty years. With a vengeance the prevalent opinion falls back to the first Seven Years' War. Dumouriez reproduces Belle-Isle and reiterates the hereditary gesture against the house of Austria. It is the Bourbons who are charged with having, since 1756, misunderstood the trend of international politics; let us wait for what the Revolution is going to do in their place. And if the King adheres to the

Treaty of Versailles, to that unnatural alliance with the Habsburg, his treason will be consumed, for, Revolution and the hatred of Austria are not to be separated. The two ideas are strictly connected : " The rupture of the alliance is as necessary as the capture of the Bastille, " says, in 1792, a member of the diplomatic committee. And Custine[1] : " To be free, we must destroy the house of Austria. " " The alliance of 1756 is incompatible with the French Constitution, " is Brissot's opinion. And later, Dumouriez states : " I have fulfilled my duty in breaking the treaty of Vienna, source of all our evils. " Real obsession for these minds which boasted of their supposed emancipation.

At the same time, they indulge in their illusions about Prussia always considered as a natural ally of France. In 1790, Ephraïm, Frederick-William's agent in Paris, mentions La Fayette, Barnave and the greater part of the leaders of the Revolutionary movement " as warmly inclined towards Prussian friendship. " The tribune of the Assem-

1. Adam-Philippe, Count of Custine. French General.

blies did not cease to echo with the praise of Frederick II and of the Hohenzollerns. Still more : to whom did the men of the Revolution, when resolved to fight Austria, offer the command of their troops? To the Duke of Brunswick himself, to him, who was, a few months later, to enter France preceded by his famous manifesto. And why had Brunswick been thought of? Because, being a kinsman of the Hohenzollern, he was looked upon as a friend of France. What a reception when the King of Prussia was seen becoming an ally of the Habsburg, — like liberal England whose benevolences could no longer be relied upon, — and rushing into the fray. A diplomatic document referred with *naïveté* to the " unnatural association which His Imperial Majesty had just formed with the King of Prussia," And Dumouriez still pleaded for the Hohenzollern while the Prussian soldiers were already crossing the frontier. It is Leopold who has excited " the successor of the immortal Frederick against France," he declared to the Assembly. This predilection for Prussia, the maintenance of constant relations with her leads us to understand the sudden Prussian retreat after the cannonade at Valmy.

" To return to the great French traditions was his heart's dream as a Frenchman, " so was said of Dumouriez. These traditions were hatred against Austria and the cult of Prussia. And this fixed idea of a return to the past, of a restoration of the ancient policy had logically to drive to Revolutionary consequences : the head of that King who will not return to the " great traditions " shall be cut off. The accusation of high treason will not be long before being thrust against him. Already the men who aim at the establishment of a Republic perceive in Louis XVI's resistance to war the factor favorable to an opportunity for putting an end to royalty.

From the very day when the idea, which was immediately popular, of a war against the house of Austria, was launched, it was fatal to be suspected of fidelity to the ancient alliance. Louis XVI, supported by the Minister of Foreign Affairs, Lessart, opposed this undertaking with all his might. Salutary opposition, indeed : it is that resistance which saved France by delaying hostilities until she had troops more or less ready for the fighting-line. "Facing an army disorganized under the regimen of Duportail, the coalition, instead of being stopped at Valmy, would have easily taken the road to Paris, and France would only have known peace again, after her humiliation and dismemberment... "

"And, moreover, in fetters, " adds an historian who is entirely favorable to the Revolution and to whom these lines are due. Thus, it would have depended only upon Louis XVI (if he had, as he was accused of, wished to buy the crushing of the Revolutionary upheaval, at the cost of France's defeat), to precipitate the war, according to the will of the Legislative, instead of delaying it.

The day Lessart was arrested and sent before a high court for what was called his " weakness towards Austria, " that very day marked the beginning of the Terror. Lessart had to be massacred in the September days.

To deserve the qualification of " Austrian " became the worst of all anathema. The " Austrian " Cabinet was overthrown, to be replaced by a " patriotic " one. The " Austrian committee " of the Tuileries was denounced as guilty of a plot against the country, And the accusation hit the King, hit the Queen, sister of the Emperor, and born in the house of the hereditary enemy. — the " Austrian, " to sum all up in a word, which was to cost her her life. During Lessart's trial, Vergniaud[1], for the first time, threw the terrible insinuation against the royal family. " From this tribune, where I speak, " cried he to the Assembly, " I see the palace where perverted counsellors mislead and blind the King whom the Constitution gave us and prepare manœuvres intended to betray us to the house of Austria. I see the windows of the palace where they are weaving the counter-revolution. " Austria and counter-revolution, the two ideas are henceforth bound together.

1. French political man and celebrated orator during the Revolution. 1753-1793.

Probably there is no Frenchman, however warm a royalist he may be, who does not feel uneasy when it appears to him that, once war declared on Austria, the Court of France still continued its relations with the Court of Vienna. One needs to reflect to realize that, at the Tuileries, Austria did not cease to be considered as an ally, that there, no enemies were recognized in Vienna, and that a war, under such conditions, seemed a disastrous absurdity. Let us imagine that a Chamber enflamed by subversive passions, had, in the month of April 1914, determined to break the Franco-Russian alliance and resolved in principle a war against autocratic Russia. M. Poincaré and a group of Republican statesmen would have opposed this act of madness. They would have kept up their good understanding with their Petrograd allies. If the Revolutionary movement in France had taken a dangerous turn, they would probably have found it quite natural to apply to Emperor Nicholas for help against anarchy. Things passed in exactly the same manner for Louis XVI and for Austria. A few im-

prudent words from Marie-Antoinette are of
no account and the grievance of treason was a
nonsense. Marie-Antoinette was in the wrong
like all women who meddle in politics without
using the suitable terms, who transform them
directly into the realm of sentiment and present them under the colors of passion.

Were they really traitors, did they intend
to deliver France to the enemy, those mode-
rate revolutionaries, those fashionable consti-
tutionalists, as were, for instance, the brothers Lameth, who had sat at the famous
" Austrian Committee ? " Their plan has
been defined in the following manner by an
historian who is neither hostile to the Revolution nor even involved in our quarrels[1].
" They had come to an understanding with
the Emperor esteeming that, as an ally of
France, it was in his interest to re-establish
order and put an end to a Revolution useful
to England and Prussia alone. They had
opposed war with all their might, and when
it had been declared, they had tried, cer-

1. A foreigner, Mr. Goetz-Bernstein, author of a study upon
the Diplomacy of the Gironde, 1912.

tainly, not to give France up to the enemy, but to return peace to her by means of negotiation with the Emperor to secure for her a quiet and steady rule and restore her former power by crushing, with the moral support on the Court of Vienna, the zealots on both sides. " Louis XVI and Marie-Antoinette had no other wish and no other plan than had these men of the golden mean.

The Girondins knew in their turn the bitterness of being accused of high treason, when Dumouriez[1], their great man, turned over to the Austrians. Henceforth, upon the destiny of the Revolution, upon the course of her policy, upon the tendencies and decisions of her diplomacy and, consequently, upon the fate of France, an invincible preference for Prussia shall bear its weight, while, towards Austria, enmity will prevail, embittered by the rancor of our civil wars, by execration of the power which symbolized the cause of the priests and of the Kings. Like Dumouriez,

1. French General who won the battles of Valmy and Jemmapes (1792).

and like Brissot, Danton [1] will call Prussia
" our natural ally. " It is with Prussia that
the Revolution, which was inconsolable over
the misunderstanding of 1791, will endeavor
to make a pact; it is Prussia that she will try
to detach from the coalition. The *Comité de
Salut public* will send the following instructions
to Barthélemy, for the peace of Bâle : " It is
quite time that Germany should be delivered
from the Austrian oppression, and that this
house, whose ambition has been. since three
centuries, the scourge of Europe, should cease
to trouble her rest. In meditating over the
State of Europe, you will surely have recognized that Prussia and France have to join
against the common foe. It is the principal
end of the negotiations in view, the one you
must try to attain. "

With still more *naïveté*, in another cir-
cumstance, the *Comité* had said : " We insist
on requiring that the principal ally of the
most powerful Republic in the world, be the
most powerful monarch in Europe. " And

1. Celebrated statesman of the Revolution. Member of
the *Comité de Salut public* (1759-1794).

if the King of Prussia refuses, if he continues obstinate, let him beware : he will be
defeated. Napoleon will boast one day of
having executed that threat.

Before marrying a Habsburg, Napoleon,
the continuator and, above all, the realizer of
the Revolutionary dreams, had shown, in its
full force, the anti-Austrian prejudice. The
master of France, at the beginning of the xix^{th}
century, had formed his mind in the last years
of the ancient regimen. The flame which the
taste for opposition and for novelties communicates to youth, marked with its brand the
policy of the mature man. Napoleon who,
on sailing for Egypt, had taken among his
favorite authors, Raynal with him, was ani-
mated against Austria by the same rancor as
Brissot in 1792. It was he who, one day,
pronounced that peculiar, and so weighty
sentence : '' The Revolution had to avenge
Prussia for the Seven Years' War sustained by
Frederick against the monstrous alliance of
France with Austria. ''   After Austerlitz,
once Austria had been vanquished, the popularity of Napoleon in France was at its zenith.

The French people believed that the old national work, undertaken under François I, had fully achieved its aim.

After that victory some emigrants began to rally round the Emperor. It became for Las Cases the origin of a legendary attachment. And Napoleon himself knew well what he had done in directing his blows against Austria, in refusing to listen to Talleyrand when advised by him to spare that power. In 1805, while exposing to Haugwitz the reasons for which he aimed at friendship with Prussia, he showed him that union between France and Austria would be the easiest thing in the world. " Only, " he added, significantly, " this alliance is not to the taste of my country and I respect that taste more than is supposed. " Napoleon flattered this " taste " of the nation, the great passion of 1792, to such a degree by crushing Austria, that, when not long ago, a celebrated anti-militarist writer suggested " hoisting the flag in the dung-hill, " a veteran of democracy, M. Camille Pelletan, reproached him for having chosen the flag of Wagram, the symbol of the victories of liberty over the reactionary powers.

Thus, the Revolution and the Empire pretended to do better than the Monarchy, or rather to restore in its purity the ancient national and royal policy anterior to 1756. It is in this sense that it was said that the Revolution had continued the ancient regimen. It continued it, no doubt, but in the wrong way, adhering obstinately to the letter of a tradition whose spirit it misunderstood. Its blunder seriously endangered the work, accomplished and spoilt the result of the successful efforts pursued by several generations of Frenchmen. With the subtle and complex net-work of the Westphalian Treaties, it infused its principle of unity. By its propaganda, it awoke in Germany the idea of nationalism. By its brutal and unrestricted annexations, by the vexations due to war and conquest, it cast the pacific reign of French influence and civilization to oblivion and fostered a great blast of revenge. It did, in a word, all that it should have carefully avoided to prevent the Germans from leaguing against us, and, for France's sake, to remove the peril of a greater Germany.

The policy of the Monarchy had aimed at dividing Germany and at keeping her in anarchical dispersion. The Revolution and the Empire assembled the pieces of this mosaic. The Revolutionaries and Napoleon, their brother by spirit, were shocked at the confusion created by the Treaties of Westphalia. This confusion, admired by Oxenstirn, appeared hideous to them, and hurt their mania for unity. In the Germanic liberties, in the mixture of principalities and of free cities, they saw but odious feudal reminiscences. " We do not understand a word of the interests of the Germanic commonwealth, " said Sieyès[1] to the Prussian Gervinus; it is for us a chaos without a single reasonable and clear idea. " Above all, what Sieyès did not perceive, was that this supposed chaos had been skilfully formed in the interest of France and for the tranquillity of Europe. This

1. Abbé Sieyès. Celebrated Statesman of the Revolution (1748-1836).

famous builder of Constitutions had no rest until he had put on foot a new plan for Germany, elaborated "a new federation more soundly and vigorously constituted than the one which chance had blindly brought forth in the Gothic centuries." Before Sieyès could be allowed to attribute to chance "the masterpiece so thoroughly studied by Richelieu and by the political men of the xviith century, it was necessary that the great traditions," to which the Revolution boasted of having returned, should be peculiarly ignored. Indeed, Sieyès was undoing conscientiously all the stipulations of the Westphalian Treaties. He was uniting what they had divided. Above all, he announced the policy which was to be that of the Napoleons, the policy of "big agglomerations" whose foundations had been planned by the Convention and the Directory, when they bought the territorial extension of France along the Rhine at the cost of "compensations" granted to the principal German powers.

This policy precipitated the stages, doubled

the doses. It made annexations, and only too rapidly, in a precarious, imprudent and costly manner, without calculating the counter-effects of these operations. Everything that experience had taught the diplomacy of the ancient regimen to avoid, the diplomacy of the new regimen adopted as though it were a discovery of its own genius. Barthélemy, one of the monarchy's agents who had been formed at the school of Vergennes, and who had continued to serve France after the death of Louis XVI, was almost alone to foresee what had to come out of that increase of the strong at the expense of the weak. " Then, " said he, but in vain, " the system which threatens Europe with the greatest of dangers will be realized, namely : the destruction and conquest of all the small States. Europe will be more enslaved than ever; war will be more terrible, liberty will be more than ever suppressed. "

In recompense for these warnings, of which we recognize the wisdom to-day, but which, at the time, were too suggestive of the hated nobility, Barthélemy, who was reputed as a

" reactionary, " was to be, shortly afterwards, deported to Guyana.

Bonaparte professed great contempt for the ideology of Sieyès. Nevertheless, it was the great scheme of reorganization of the German commonwealth, as imagined by this ideologist, that Napoleon achieved. His victories served him to model Germany- on a plan which led him to foresee a reconstitution of the German unity and paved the way to this unity. Through the " recess " of 1803, result of the victory of Hohenlinden, Bonaparte struck the first blow to the edifice erected in 1648. He considerably simplified the federal system of the Holy Empire by the secularisation of nearly all the ecclesiastical principalities, and by the suppression of the greater number of the free cities among which only six in fifty subsisted. As Alfred Rambaud distinctly said, a real revolution took place in Germany which reproduced all the principles of ours. " The German Revolution of 1803 was practically as radical as the French Revolution. At Ratisbonne, as in Paris, the sovereign nobility, and the independent municipalities were destroyed. At Ratisbonne, as in Paris, the ecclesiastical estates were secularized. At Ratisbonne as in Paris, more unity and centralisation were obtained." But, while it was sterilizing to France, this centralizing evolution was beneficient for Germany, and brought her nearer to the form of a normal State. Three years later, Austerlitz permitted Napoleon to complete his enterprise. This new victory of our armies marked a new step for Germany along the path which was to save her from parcelling and anarchy.. The Emperor believed he was using the cleverest diplomacy. In fact, he was inspired by school maxims, by a quantity of sentiments and ideas he had acquired in his early youth. He was continuing, or, rather, achieving the foreign policy that he had inherited from the Revolution, the system of excessive and brutal conquests which were to be bought at the expense of the weakest, and turned to the advantage of the strongest.

The " recess, " or remodelling of 1806 gave, or nearly gave to Germany, the physiognomy which she was to assume during the xix[th] century. By the mediatisation of numberless small sovereignties blended into others which were increased, he left only about thirty States which, except for a few changes, were in our time to form a Germany united under the rule of Prussia. Such was the consequence of Austerlitz.

It was not only the territorial Constitution which was overthrown, but the political Constitution, also. With Austerlitz, the Holy Empire falls down. The Habsburgs would no longer, of course, be Emperors in Germany, and the wish of French opinion, when, in 1741, enthusiastic at the idea of doing away with the house of Austria as a German power, that wish was to be fulfilled. There will be no Emperor any longer or, rather, the Emperor shall be Napoleon, the successor of Charlemagne, who will flatter himself with having revived the Carolingian Empire, who will make himself King of Italy, and crown his heir King of Rome, just as the Germanic Cæsars named their sons Kings of the Romans. But, when Napoleon had been thrown down and his phanstasmagoria had been dissipated, the old elective and anarchical institutions of the Empire do not reappear, the place will be free for a new Empire and there will be but few chances of any return of the conditions which had caused the political impotence of Germany. " That dear, Holy Empire, how does it still survive? " So sing, in Gœthe's " Faust, " the roisterers in the tavern. However old it was, it lasted, just as when we had put it in bonds, and paralyzed it in 1648. The French should have been the last to abolish it. By throwing it down, they destroyed one of the principal guarantees of their own security.

The Revolution accomplished beyond the Rhine by our armies and our legislators did not only have its effect upon the political and territorial constitution of the German States. Another Revolution, not less serious, had taken place in all minds, similar to the French Revolutionary movement. Historians agree to-day in saying that the ideas of 1789, spread through the Germanies by our soldiers there, awakened the sentiment of nationalities. " In Germany, Jean-Jacques Rousseau[1] ", said Dubois-Reymond (a very Prussophile writer, like all the descendants of the refugees after the revocation of the Edict of Nantes) in a curious passage : " Jean-Jacques Rousseau was received like a Christopher Columbus. ". Germany recognized herself in the books of the philosopher of Geneva, whose doctrines, consubstantial with Germanism, were imported, or rather, brought back, and spread by the armed propagandists of the French Revolution. " German patriotism springs from the Rights of Man, " remarks Albert Sorel. It springs thence through the most natural filiation.

The principle of nationalities is the true expression of the Revolutionary philosophy. It is in strict connexion with the principle of popular sovereignty. Every nation is considered as composed of individuals endowed with sacred and imprescriptible rights. The

---

1. Philosopher and French writer, born at Geneva (Switzerland) 1712-1778. Author of : *Le Contrat Social*, *Émile*, *La Nouvelle Héloïse*, etc...

doctrine of the Revolution will, therefore, attribute to every nation the same right as to the individuals which compose it. Every nation shall be considered as though it were a person. Its character and its liberties shall be respected, for nations are equal in regard of one another as are individuals. Every nation, therefore, has the right to live and grow according to its nature; and the idea imported by Jean-Jacques Rousseau is that everything which is natural is beautiful, just and divine. In that idea Germany finds herself and conceives herself with admiration. Proceeding to the cosmopolitanism of the xviii[th] century, when one of her " intellectuals, " Lessing[1], stated that he had no idea of what consisted the love for the " fatherland, " when the superiority of the French civilization was not contested, and when, according to general agreement, it was realizing the unity of the European commonwealth, thinking Germany passes to the most enflamed nationalism through the transition

1. German writer (1729-1781).

of Rousseau adjusted to Germanism by Herder.

Here we touch upon one of those points where the action of ideas duplicates the action of events, where the spiritual, by its conjunction with the temporal, drives their policy's axioms to extreme limits. The Terror had its origin in the humanitarian dogmas of the Revolution. A scourge, still more hideous, its offspring too, Germanism, was in sight. To-day, of course, the sons of the Revolution close their eyes with shame : " The wave which brought it, recedes horrified. " Nevertheless, the responsibility of his ideas, as certain as that of the men, shines here with the force of evidence.

Herder[1], nurtured on Rousseau's teaching, professes a cosmopolitanism in which the great conflicts of nationalities and races are in germ. That cosmopolitanism is summed up in the statement that there is, in all people, a something precious and sacred, which noone is entitled to encroach upon : it is the

1. Gottfried Herder, German philosopher (1744-1803).

national stamp, the soul of the race. Language, which is the expression of that soul, serves, consequently, to define national individuality. Hence, it is every nation's strict duty to give to its own personality its fullest development. This idea was wonderfully new and pregnant with great novelties in a Germany endlessly parcelled and to whom national existence had been denied more than to any other country. The Germans had lost the idea that they could ever exist as a nation. That idea, the Revolution brought it to them, but peculiarly aggravated.

Jean-Jacques Rousseau had taught the principle of the return to Nature. He had taught that, the younger and newer a people, the more of good is in it; that, the less advanced in civilization, the more virtuous. This teaching was adopted by the Germans with enthusiasm. It avenged and rehabilitated Germany whose contribution to general civilization had, until then, been almost non-existent : of this sterility, she was proud as of a virginity. To this we owe the legends about a pure and virtuous Germany in which France, following in the footsteps of Mme de Staël[1], so long believed. Herder, and later Fichte, and the promotors of a national revival of Germany, made use of these precepts. They taught that Germany's turn had come; that she had not only her destiny to fulfill, but also her mission to accomplish. The German people will henceforth be the predestined people, the people of the Lord, the one whose task will be to lead the world into the path of morality and progress. This theme is the one we know so well : it is that of *Kultur*, that of the appeal of the 93 German intellectuals, the essential principle which has exalted the Germany of our days, which impelled her to the war of 1914, to the invasion of France and of Belgium to the domination of Europe.

Already in 1794, a Nuremberg writer called Ehrard, wrote : " Will not the Germans at last defend their rights themselves? I am not an aristocrat, but I cannot allow that

1. Daughter of Necker, minister of Finances under Louis XVI. — Celebrated for her writings (1766-1817).

French judgment should pretend to tutorship over my German judgment." Thus the Revolution had no sooner enfranchized the German spirit, then this spirit took the offensive against its liberators by a natural move. The doctrines of the Revolution, when spreading beyond France, turned against us in this manner. Once launched by our own victories all over a dismantled and disorganized Europe, the principle of nationalities, ferment of future struggles for the constitution of German unity, was going to bring to the imprudent and unfortunate French a long sequence of calamities.

1813, 1815, the " battle of the nations, " Waterloo, the conquests lost, the Napoleonic Empire thrown down like a house of cards, France invaded : all this is the sequence of a great drama, it is the popular war willed and provoked by the men of the Revolution, the war of 1792 which closes. For, since the rupture with Austria, the work of the legislative, until Napoleon's last battle, it was all one and the same war, which, after twenty-three years of tragedies, millions of lives sacrificed, ended in our defeat and left us, for all consolation, but a capital of glory. Then, the descendant of Hugues Capet came back to save what could be saved, to start again on the family work of his forefathers. Patiently, he does his best to re-weave the texture. Full of courage, Louis XVIII assumes the liquidation of the heavy inheritance he has found. With striking brevity, Proudhon has said, when speaking of 1815 : " Like convicts, the unfortunate Bourbons once more shoulder their task ! " Ungrateful task, indeed, and which was to receive its reward in calumny and exile.

The treaties of 1816 have, during the greatest part of the xix[th] century, been an object of hatred and horror for French patriotism. From fear of public opinion the Governments, who conformed their action to these treaties, did not dare to invoke them and only alluded to them with diffidence. Thiers said they were to be hated, though respected, and Guizot, that they were to be respected while being hated. The last volumes of the *Histoire du*

Consulat et de l'Empire, by Thiers, published
in 1860-1862, again present a fierce criticism
of the Treaties of Vienna, from the national
point of view.   When, in 1863, Napoleon III
declared that the Treaties of 1815 had ceased
to exist, it was with the applause of the multitude who, on this occasion even more heartily and more thoughtlessly in France than
elsewhere, cried : " Hurrah for my death. "

The cruel lessons of 1870 were necessary
to give another course, not to public opinion,
always slow in placing itself on a level with
reason and science, but to the judgments of
History.   Compared to the Treaty of Francfort, the treaties of Vienna appeared such as
they were : masterpieces of diplomacy by
which the effects of crushing disasters were
repaired as well as possible.   With shocking
ingratitude, public opinion charged the Bourbons with the penalty of the very defeats
which the reign of opinion had caused, and
for which the idol of opinion was responsible.
If there is any example which teaches the
great political men that they must work for
the masses without the slightest hope of being

rewarded or even understood, it is that one. And it is again, in our history, a new matter for scandal that the French should so violently have hated the Treaties which, in the detestable condition where the Revolution and the Empire had left them, returned to them, nearly intact in its former limits, the territory that the conquerors intended to divide.

Moreover, these treaties removed from us the peril of seeing threatening powers close to our doors. Learned books have, in our days, recognized that the negotiations of 1814 and 1815 had been masterfully conducted. Still, the return from the Island of Elba, the fatal weakness of Ney[1], and the defeat of Waterloo did not make them easy. If Louis XVIII and his genial tactician, Talleyrand, are not mentioned as models, it is rather late and the evil is done. Louis XVIII and Talleyrand have been scorned and libelled, equally by great poets and by petty journalists. The services rendered to France by these two men

1. Marshall of France. Duc d'Elchingen, Prince de la Moskowa. 1769-1815. Napoleon called him : " The bravest of the brave. "

were miserably ignored.   In our days, even, it is nearly in vain that one of the historians who have wished to rehabilitate the work of 1815, has written : " Does one conceive France, the day after the war of 1870, concluding with Saxony, Bavaria and Wurtemberg a treaty of alliance against Prussia? Does one imagine what moral force this compact would have procured for us, what confidence this diplomatic revenge on our military defeats would have brought back to us? It is a privilege of this kind that France of 1814 owed to Talleyrand. " And, let us also add, to Louis XVIII, whose correspondence shows with what clearsightedness he directed the negotiations of Vienna.   How sad it is for the reputation of such an intelligent people as is the French, among whom each citizen is really endowed with the best of good sense and shows ability for his private interests, that a third invasion and a third disaster should have been necessary before they began to understand, and even then, only among the elite, that, what had been effectuated in 1815, was the reparation of

the errors and follies of a whole generation!

The greatest, the most useful result obtained by Louis XVIII was to prevent the part
taken by Prussia in the defeat of the Napoleonic Empire from ending in the formation
of a grest Germany. In taking sides for
Saxony in the name of the principle of legitimacy, skilfully turned against the Allies to
whom it had served as a pretext against Revolutionary and Napoleonic France, the King of
France had recuperated, at the same time, the
high European standing of his predecessors.
He had come forth as the protector and the
syndic of the middle or small states, and had,
immediately, grouped a circle of depen-
dents and allies about him and rebuilt the
ancient diplomatic system of France. Having
discerned the ambition of Prussia, the Bourbon succeeded in baffling the plans of the
Hohenzollern. Thanks to him, when statutes
were to be given to Germany, the principle
of independence and sovereignty of the Germanic States laid down by the Treaties of
Westphalia was again ratified at Vienna.

That is to say that Germany, as was essential, remained divided.

Unfortunately, it was no longer possible to re-form the simplifications and agglomerations established in 1803 and 1806. Instead · of several hundreds of sovereign States, only about forty were left. Instead of being unrestrictedly morcelled, Germany was, henceforth, distributed into a certain number of big provinces. But these provinces were self-governed and had no common chief. The federative bond which united them was as loose, as slight as that of the Holy Empire. The Diet of Francfort, which was the expression of that bond, was the theater of the quarrels and rivalries of particularism, causing the despair and shame of the German unitarian patriots. The unification of Germany, which had for a short time passed before their eyes, was again impossible. The German Republic, reconstituted at Vienna, was to be, until 1866, our safeguard on the Rhinish border.

It has often been said, and is still repeated, that the Treaties of 1815 had trampled upon the rights of the people and had breathed the reactionary spirit of Metternich [1]. Considering the true interest of France, Metternich must be judged as having been well advised, inasmuch as the most wronged people at the congress of Vienna was precisely the one which, as soon as attaining its complete rights, would at once encroach on the existence of the other nations.

For, if anyone had reason to complain of the treaties of 1815, it was assuredly Prussia. Not only was she deceived in her desire that France be divided, as she had insistently demanded, but she did not even receive the price she had stipulated for her part in the common victory. Prussia did not secure Saxony which she coveted so much, and which would have given her, with the territorial consistency she longed for, the domination over the whole of Germany. She was dissatisfied with the Rhinish provinces handed over to her but which spread her dominions still further, drew the Kingdom out of its boundaries, and brought her a lot of Catholic

1. Clement Wenceslas, prince of Metternich-Winneburg. Celebrated Austrian statesman (1773-1859).

and Latinized populations which were just as sympathetic to French civilization as they were hostile to the rule and spirit of Prussia. In this whole Rhine country the Revolution was again to explode to the cry of : " Down with Prussia. "

We have a valuable testimonial of the state of mind in the Prussian elite in 1815 ; it is the journal which Stein [1] kept of his impressions during the Congress of Vienna. Stein has expressed the deception and bitterness of the patriots and of the reformers who, by energetic and patient effort, had helped the Prussians after the catastrophe of Iena and who, by taking the lead in the war of independence and of the nationalist movement against the Napoleonic occupation, had reckoned that their country would super-impose itself over Germany to accomplish the national unity. The disappointment caused by the Treaties of 1815 was so extensive and has remained so acute that, in our days, a Prussian has been able to write that the French had turned their defeats of

1. Henry, Baron von Stein. German statesman (1756-1831).

1814 and of 1815 into a victory over Prussia, and that Waterloo had, in the end, been a practical success for France. This expression, of course, must not be taken too literally ; but it throws light on the true character of the Treaties of Vienna of which Stein also said that they had closed the German national upheaval of 1813 with a farce. Moreover, outside Prussia, the German patriots who had derived their new sentiments and aspirations towards a great Germany from the ideas of the century and in the exhortations of Fichte, hated these Treaties in no less degree.

German patriots suffered acutely from the Treaties of Vienna which indefinitely put off he hopes that the war of liberation and the great patriotic wave through Germany of 1813 had raised.   Ranke[1] wrote, in 1832 : " Never has our country been divided into so many pieces and morsels which are quite foreign to each other. Never have principalities enjoyed a similar independence and never

1. German historian (1795-1886).

have princes and subjects been more jealous
of it. "   Ranke showed, also, that the new
customs introduced into the heart of the
States by the new Charts and by the genera-
lization of the parliamentary regimen still
added to the former causes of discord, the
causes of permanent disorder called parties.
Henceforth, there was opposition in Germany
not only between the States devoted to particularisms, not only between Catholics and
Protestants, but also between liberals and
conservatives.   In facing this revival of the
old Germanic anarchy in a new shape, Ranke
despaired of the future and forsook the German
dream : " Must we not, " cried he, losing his
illusions, " give up for ever all hope of
founding the German unity ? "

One conceives therefore that the German
patriots had serious reasons for detesting the
Holy Alliance and the " tyrants " sworn
against their independence.   Their hatred
was as justified as was that of the Italian
patriots.   It went as far as taking the way of
direct action, as far as propaganda through
facts.   But the French ?   By what error have

they nourished the same passion ? Did they not keep the possibility, under favor of eventual circumstances, of taking back the frontier of the Rhine, these necessary frontiers one moment won, but also lost by the Revolution ? Instead of this, the French patriots, from 1815 to 1866, were filled with desire to deliver their German brothers..... Heine's[1] sarcasm in the preamble to his book, *Germany*, will in vain have taught them, that they did not see the enemy where he really was, that they raved when they fancied that Germany would feel in brotherly fashion for them, the day when " the Holy Alliance of people, " as sung Béranger, " would succeed to the Holy Alliance of Kings ". " Beware, " said Heine, " I have only good intentions, and I tell you the bitter truth. You have more to fear from a free Germany than from the whole of the Holy Alliance, with all its Croats and Cossacks "... For it is far from true that the Cossacks and the Slavs have always been, in the eyes of the French democrats, the soldiers of justice and of right.

1. Heinrich Heine. German writer and poet (1799-1856).

The thoughtless hatred of the Treaties of 1815, which was the current coin of the liberal opposition's policy in France charges the liberal school and its heir, the old Republican party, with a contradiction the historian finds inexplicable. The liberalism of the xix[th] century believed it possessed the means of founding universal peace and fraternity. It fancied that the formation of nationalities would preface the European Republic. The results obtained are derisory. They cause one to regret the past. We see to-day that the Treaty of 1815 had instituted an order of things in Europe which guaranteed peace better than the conference of The Hague was ever able to do. Referring to the principles of legitimacy and balance introduced by France in the public right of Europe, the authors of the Treaties of 1815 had declared that, henceforth, any aggrandizement of a state at the expense of another was prohibited. Whosoever should threaten the established equilibrium would be regarded as a revolutionary and the disturber of European order, in the same way as was Napoleon, and would be exposed to see the whole of Europe join against him. An international police-force was sorely lacking in France and in Europe, in 1870. While restoring the principle of equilibrium proclaimed in 1648, the Treaties of 1815 had organized this police and it is simply to 1815 and to 1648 that the coalition formed in 1914 against the German Empire aims at returning. The European equilibrium of the xixth century was defined by Gentz, the writer on the Holy Alliance and in such a way that one can imagine oneself hearing a speech by Sir Edward Grey, by M. Vandervelde or by M. Viviani : " The best guarantee of the general peace is the firm will of each power to respect the rights of its neighbours, and the well-announced resolution of all to make *common cause* against the one who, disregarding this principle, should trespass on the boundaries fixed by a political system invested with the universal sanction. " (Project of a final declaration of the eight powers who signed the final act of the Congress of Vienna.)

It is in virtue of the Treaties of 1815 that

the federal execution against Prussia was pronounced in 1866.   If France had then contributed to respect the compact of 1815, Bismarck, on being treated like Napoleon, would have been stopped in his conquests. The first power called upon to benefit by a coalition against Prussia, we are but too well aware of it, would have been France.

The Holy Alliance, with its periodical congresses for the settlement of European affairs, has realized the most serious effort ever seen in modern times for the guarantee of peace in Europe.   This international understanding was based on the principle of preservation and which France, in the interests of her own welfare, ought never to have tampered with.

On the contrary, it was France, with Napoleon III's government, a government born from public opinion, who impaired the Treaties of 1815 and inaugurated a policy of nationalities against them.   We know what came of it : our defeats, the mutilation of our territory, our decline, the greatness of the rival powers, and, in 1914, a war more terrible

than all the others, with a fifth invasion.
The middle of the xixth century, from this
point of view, is a significant date in European affairs whose effects even reach the
United States.   The German unity which, in
1815, had become again chimerical, re-enters,
after 1848, the sphere of possibilities.   It
remains to be seen how the dynasty of the
Hohenzollerns dealt with the errors and faults
of France in order to make Germany a power
united and ominous for all the nations of the
world.

CHAPTER V

" THE POLICY ELABORATED BY THE PEOPLE
SINCE 1815, " LEADS US TO SEDAN

The *Confession d'un Enfant du Siècle*, by
Alfred de Musset[1], has transfixed the image
of the " ardent, pale, nervous generation "
of those Frenchmen conceived between two
battles and which reached its full adolescence
at the time of Waterloo.   It is precisely
that France which suffered mostly from what
has been so rightly called the " malady of
1815. "   This evil, similar to the famous
Romantic evil, had the same causes.   It was
a mixture of lively yet confused aspirations,
mingling with the traditions of glory and of

1. French poet (1810-1857).

liberty with the souvenirs of the Revolution and of the Empire, with the shock felt in all the fibres as a result of the marvellous adventures that France had been going through for twenty-five years. The prostration of the final defeat added an element of bitterness and of revolt to the state of sensibility. Between this medley of enthusiasm and of nervosity, and the realism of the political men of the *Restauration*, a disagreement could not fail to arise. On this misunderstanding the attempt to renew the confidence between France and the Bourbons was stranded.

The monarchy, after having raised France, which it then found so low, was entitled to rely on the possibility of pursuing its task, if not on the French nation's gratitude. It did not wait for this reward before beginning to work for the general welfare. A word of rancor was never uttered by the Bourbons. Charles X, that much-diffamed King, and of whom M. Émile Ollivier[1] was enabled to say

1. French Statesman. Minister of Napoleon III (1826-1913).

that he was " aflame for the national revival, " retook the road of exile without manifesting a shadow of the surprise and sorrow expressed by his minister Villèle, when he said that the *Restauration* had put France back in her place in Europe, giving her again order, rest, prosperity, though France did not seem to be aware of these benefits.

We, at this distance, are also inclined to wonder that France, after Waterloo, was not worn out by her long years of war and useless conquests. It was reasonable to believe that the *Restauration* would have enabled the country to enjoy the tranquillity recovered, without sacrificing any lasting profits or military glory : the expeditions of Spain, Greece and Algeria could well suffice to a people even so spoiled in the matter of warlike exploits. But it would have been reckoning without the policy of the parties, already regularly established. France had no sooner emerged from the liquidation of the Empire, then the parties took hold of the foreign policy, as of the most efficacious and murderous arm in the daily conflicts. The

relations of the State with the exterior
becoming an occasion for civil war, a pretext
of opposition, or of action, it was the
country herself, with her interests and her
security, which was reduced to the level of
stakes in the electoral and parliamentary
battle. This was seen from the beginning
of the *Restauration*. It is in this privileged
and sacred domain of foreign policy that the
most lively campaign was sustained against
Louis XVIII and Charles X. And why this
choice? It is because the parties of the opposition felt themselves supported by the
patriotic sentiment mislead and mistaken
about itself by revolutionary and Napoleonic
recollections. To flatter what has been called
" the mania of glory and of conquest " was
the enterprise to which the opposition devoted
itself, on the pretext that France was humiliated by the treaties of 1815, and put in tow
of the absolutist powers, and on the pretext
of the monarchy rewarding the foreigner
(according to an absurd but efficicacious
legend) for the services received from him.
Without considering what the *Restauration*

had already done, what she intended doing to repair, time and circumstances helping, the final consequences of Waterloo, the men of the liberal opposition did not hesitate to use this arm, provided it served their personal ambition, increased their popularity, and contributed to their glory.

The surprise which the rage of his adversaries, amongst whom were some legitimists, caused the wise Villèle[1], came from his very wisdom itself. This excellent minister, this administrator of sound sense, did not take any account of the " malady of 1815, " of the demon tormenting the French, driving them to work against their most evident interests. Other royalists, who were themselves " enfants du siècle, " who found Louis XVIII's work prosaic, cherished, at that very moment, the idea that the Monarchy could and should adopt the program of revolutionary patriotism : i. e. nationalities and conquests. It was the policy which Chateau-

1. Comte de Villèle. French Statesman. Leader of the Ultra-Royalists. Minister of Louis XVIII and Charles X (1773-1854).

briand[1] had recommended with both eloquence and ill-humor, that which Polignac[2]
was to try to carry through.

Gifted with a fine imagination, of weak and
rather chimerical intellect, Polignac had the
intuition of a policy capable of returning a
reluctant popularity to royalty. He attempted,
but without adequate means, without the
necessary organization and preparation, what
Napoleon III was to undertake later : a policy,
conservative as regards interior affairs, gilded
by a sparkling satisfaction given, abroad, to
the liberal aspirations. The great project of
the remaking of Europe which he put on foot
with Bois-le-Comte, in the last years of the
Restauration was, in fact, impracticable, and
even frankly bad and imprudent in some of
its workings, especially those, where, planning to remodel the German Confederation,
he repeated the errors of the revolutionary
period, and wanted to buy the Rhinish fron-

1. Famous French writer. Minister of Foreign Affairs
under the *Restauration* (1768-1848).

2. Jules-Armand, Duc de Polignac. Minister under
Charles X (1780-1847).

tier by the so dangerous system of " com-, pensations, ", which was to consummate the ruin of the second Empire. Polignac fell and his project fell with him. Neither he, nor Chateaubriand, had succeeded in convincing public opinion that a Bourbon could continue Napoleon's policy, — that of Waterloo and of Sedan. This incredulity is to-day one of the titles of the monarchy to be esteemed and regretted by the French.

At the same time as Polignac, Charles X left the stage. The curtain was also rung down on the prospects which had opened for us, and that riper and wiser minds would one day have used.

With the Revolution of 1830 were destroyed the fruits of fifteen years of patient, prudent and faultless policy. The first result of the overthrow of Charles X was to place France again in the critical position of 1814 and 1815. Facing a revolutionary France, the powers feared another war of propaganda and proselytism. The pact of Chaumont[1]

1. Treaty concluded in 1814, between the Allies, in order to reduce France to her limits in 1789.

was revived. France which, at that time, still belonged to the Holy Alliance was put on the index by a coalition of sovereigns. The Russian alliance, then under good way, disappeared not to appear again until our day. Nothing remained, neither the advantages already put to our account, nor of still brighter promises. After the days of July, everything had to be done over in order to restore France not only to her place in Europe, but to any place whatsoever. Another Bourbon, a new convict of the crown, was still there to undertake the task once more and once more to fail, confronted by the same passions, the same errors of democracy.

On the evening of July 31st 1830, when the Orléans solution began to prevail, Cavaignac, one of the heads of the Revolution, put this preliminary question to Louis-Philippe : '' What is your opinion regarding the Treaties of 1815? This is not a liberal revolution, bear it well in mind, it is a national revolution. The sight of the tricolored flag, that is what has raised the people and it would certainly be easier to drive it on from Paris to the Rhine, than from Paris to Saint-Cloud. "

These words show that the revolution of July had at its root the rancor, left by the Treaties of 1815. When they drove out Charles X, the Parisians thought less of securing political liberty than of pursuing abroad the revolutionary and Napoleonic program to which the will of Saint-Helena had lent an appearance of Gospel-truth. It was the first endeavor to impose what M. Émile Ollivier[1], who was to be its slave, had pompously named " the policy elaborated by the people since 1815. "

Chosen, " although a Bourbon " for the throne of a new constitutional monarchy, Louis-Philippe, just because he was a Bourbon, could not permit France to go to her ruin. No sooner had he begun to reign than the disagreement, the conflict sprung up again. Louis-Philippe (posterity at length has understood it) spared France a catastrophy in 1840. He saved our country in

1. Politician, Napoleon III's principal minister during the last and liberal period of the second Empire (1826-1913).

advance by helping, in 1830, to build up an independent Belgium, by having the neutrality of the new Belgian State recognized. Such was, as remarked the Duc de Broglie, the " last gift of the monarchy, " a gift of which we have just felt the value. How few Frenchmen are aware, at this moment, that they have been protected, at nearly eighty years distance, by the skilful thought of perhaps the most ridiculed of all our states. The contemporary Frenchman perceived nothing in it. His frivolity, his blindness has been appalling. The policy " that the people elaborated since 1815 " took no note of the prudent diplomatic conceptions which were one day to save the nation. Democracy was not far from seeing treason in every work of public welfare. Let her only follow her own way : in a few minutes, she will assure the greatness of France and the happiness of the people. Deplorable presumption!...

It was by exasperating the " malady of 1815, " that the Republican and Bonapartist elements, hand in hand, for, the same ticket which had made Napoleon the executor of the revolutionary program, stirred up the unpopularity of the Monarchy of July. It was the King's fault, if France was idle and humiliated in Europe : so spoke, with persuasive fire, the '' patriots who wanted war against kings. '' '' Shame, athousand shames to the impertinent and cowardly system which insists on proclaiming the political egotism of France, '' cried Armand Carrel. The phrase : '' people's cause '' intoxicated these sons of 1792. As Louis Blanc wrote, in his *Histoire de dix ans*, '' the democratic frenzy then lived more on the life of other nations than on that of France. '' It was again Louis Blanc who said : '' We lived especially in Poland. '' And not only in Poland, — democracy lived also in Italy, in Germany, everywhere, except in France. How evident it is that France had not then, at her frontiers, a vast military Empire always ready to overrun her with its millions of soldiers.

The dreams, the illusions of an ignorant crowd, of an enthusiastic and mystic youth, of leaders exalted by a life of solitary con-

templation, find perhaps an excuse in the
judgment of the Frenchmen of to-day, tou-
ched by that exaltation and by that lyricism,
although their miserable effects are so cruelly
felt. This excuse does not exist for mature
men, broken to affairs, to whom their education, their social rank should have procured
the means of acquiring experience and of resisting to the pressure of the mob. In a
Parliament not elected by universal suffrage,
but by the restrained scrutiny of the rich
and enlightened middle classes, Louis-Philippe again met the follies of the street.
They affected, however, a solemn expression.
They borrowed the language of Statesmen.
They adopted the keynote of the rostrum,
of the academies, of the drawing-rooms.
But these follies were the same, as were
those of the students. The proud doctri-
naries profoundly despised, after having
accepted their help in 1830, the rioters, the
barricaders, the petty Republican journalists.
But they shared the same errors. Above his
stiff necktie, a Duvergier de Hauranne, in
La Politique extérieure de la France, echoed

Carrel and Marrast: like them he demanded that France " should everywhere support the people against their governments, take in Europe the lead in the great revolutionary and liberal movement of which she was the head and the heart. " It is against that policy that Louis-Philippe wore himself out fighting, during eighteen years, to try to implant his wise and penetrating views on the situation of France in Europe. The task he had to fulfill, in order to maintain the equilibrium by resisting the impact of nationalities instead of favoring them, was gigantic. And for this, his famous " personal policy. " he was incessantly harassed.

The exploitation of foreign policy by theorists whose self-love would have put the world on fire, or by ambitious politicians who would have established their glory even on the ruins of their country, is the scandal of parliamentarism under the Monarchy of July. What had been seen under Charles X was peculiarly aggravated. From this point of view, the career of Thiers during the reign of Louis-Philippe must be considered with attention.   Thiers was not a doctrinaire; his mind was quick to vary; he was eager for glory and success; his intellect, marvellously lucid, was fitted to understand and to execute the base as well as the good.   In 1836, on his entry into office, the agreement with Austria, the conservative policy, the entente with the Continental powers were the order of the day. Thiers approved of this policy, made it his own peculiar business.   Louis-Philippe had the idea, in order to sustain his Bourbonian thought, of giving an Austrian Arch-Duchess as wife to his heir, the Duc of Orleans. This project became dearer to Thiers than to the King and to the young Prince themselves. Thiers swore to succeed, dreaming that with so brilliant a start, his Ministry would acquire lustre and solidity.   It happened that the Court of Austria, inspired by Metternich, declined for many reasons (amongst which Thiers' excessive haste was not without influence), the request of the son of Louis Philippe.   Thiers was more mortified about it than anybody else.   This failure was attributed to him and to his Ministry.   He retained a grudge against Metternich and soon his wounded *amour-propre* suggested a new policy. He proclaimed himself the adversary of the absolutist powers, turned towards liberal alliances and in a spirit of vengeance, he proposed a French intervention in favor of the Spanish radicals. It was then that Louis-Philippe, not hesitating to come forward again, broke Thiers, as he had broken the Duc de Broglie, to protect the interest of the country.

The whole of Louis-Philippe's reign passed in conflicts between the King, on one side, the parliamentarians and public opinion, on the other, the parliamentarians being led astray by their spirit of system, their party-spirit, their personal ambition; public opinion being misled by void declamations about the oppression of the people and revolutionary solidarity. During these eighteen years of struggle, those years during which prevailed the counsels of the Crown (of the " Castle, " as the satirists said), were also the best. But none, not even those who had made him King, credited Louis-Philippe with them, none understood the wisdom and the foresight of his policy.

In 1839, was witnessed one of the most significant manifestations of parliamentary life in the July Monarchy. Ousted party-leaders, chiefs of clans, all who were thirsting for power, or whose *amour-propre* had been hurt, combined to snatch the leadership of affairs from the King. It was the coalition put up by Broglie, by Thiers and by Guizot[1]. These three statesmen took, in equal doses, their share of responsibility in the international events of 1840, so critical for France. As under the *Restauration*, foreign policy was, above all, the weapon turned by the parties against the crown. Molé[2] fell before the "immoral and noxious coalition," and the King, whose personal power was aimed at, behind Molé, was hit by the same stroke.

That victory of partisan policy received, unhappily for France, a prompt and severe punishment. The parliamentary coalition

1. French statesman and historian (1787-1874.)
2. Louis Mathieu, Count Molé. Premier under Louis-Philippe.

charged Louis-Philippe with lacking in dignity with the foreign powers. Thus it happened that Thiers, once back in power, started an active and provocating policy whose principle was to support Mehemet-Ali[1] against the Sultan, and eventually against the whole of Europe. Thiers formed the Ministry on March 1st. 1840. On the 15th of July, France suddenly learnt that the four great powers had settled the Eastern question among themselves, without referring to her, without even giving her the slightest hint. We were back in the situation of 1830 and of 1814, with the Holy Alliance against us. The Government was supported by the people. We had, at this time, to face the revival of German nationalism, which had recovered the virulence of the Napoleonic period and of the war of Independence. Thiers had challenged Europe. He had revived recollections of the Revolution and of the Empire. He faced, without reluctance, a French war against the whole of Europe, an absurd war,

1. Vice-Roy of Egypt. Sustained two wars against Turkey in 1832 and 1839. (1769-1849.)

indeed, but which would have raised him to glory, whatever its issue. He was found in his library, lying flat over maps on which, like Bonaparte, he prepared his battles. War was, once more, prevented by Louis-Philippe who, resisting public opinion at the risk of passing for pusillanimous, and, not hesitating to unveil himself, repaired the faults of his parliamentary Minister. Louis-Philippe had courageously affronted the current which was carrying France into an unequal fight against the rest of Europe. He did not fear to expose his personality, to forsake his constitutional neutrality, to face unpopularity by opposing what he rightly said would be the struggle of one against four. But Thiers, having tendered his resignation to the King who was denying him " his war, " Louis-Philippe did not wish it to be said that even the Minister whose policy he did not approve, had quitted the Cabinet under a foreign threat. It was Thiers again who, in October of 1840, proceeded to the preliminaries of a very honorable settlement by which Mehemet-Ali, in exchange for the restoration of Syria, received

the hereditary investiture of Egypt that the
Powers in July were ready to take from him.
Thiers left office after a parliamentary speech
in which, by a last bravado and to mask his
failure, he was once more pleased to challenge
the whole of Europe[1].

The Monarchy had saved France from a
disastrous war, from a Waterloo or a Sedan
into which the blindness of opinion, aggravated by the *amour-propre* of the parliamentary chiefs, exploited by the regime of
parties, would have thrown her. However,
the war-like enterprise into which Thiers,
from vanity, would have launched a whole
nation, left in Europe a fermentation dangerous for France. In Germany nationalism
seemed disposed to be fanatical. Metternich
observed it with his usual penetration and

1. One will find in the third volume of the " Manuel de
Politique étrangère, " by Émile Bourgeois, a just appreciation
of the rôle played by the Monarchy of July in this crisis.
M. Bourgeois, among many other quotations which are to
the honor of Louis-Philippe, relates this retort of Guizot's :
" An immense favor rendered to the country, a service
analogous to those which the Crown has already rendered
her several times, in similar circumstances. "

haughty irony : " M. Thiers, " said he, " likes to be compared to Napoleon. Well, as far as Germany is concerned, the resemblance is perfect and the palm must even be given to M. Thiers. But a short time sufficed him to bring that country to the point where ten years of oppression had brought it under the Emperor. "

And Heine's did not differ from the judgment of the technician of the Holy Alliance : " M. Thiers, " wrote he, " with his noisy drumming, woke our good Germany up from her lethargic sleep, and pushed her into the great whirl of European politics. He beat the drum so loudly that we could not go to sleep again, and since then, we have remained on our feet. If we ever become a nation, M. Thiers will be able to say that he did nothing to prevent it and German history will credit him with this achievement. " These lines were printed in 1854. Sixteen years later, events proved Heine to be right : it was Sedan.

In France the warning of 1840 did not pass entirely unheeded. One of the accom-

plices " of the immoral and fatal coalition "
realized the extent of his fault. Later he even
recognized it publicly. It was Guizot.
Guizot, forsaking Thiers and the parliamentarians, giving up a low partisan policy, was,
henceforth, to work with Louis-Philippe to
repair the evil he had caused. He was the
Molé[1] of the Second period of the reign. It
is just, also, to say that the Duc de Broglie was one of the first, to take notice of the
severe lesson given by Europe. that he
renounced his doctrinaire stiffness, and
endeavored to help the King to avert the peril.

All had to be done over again in order
to give to France her true national policy, a
policy of safety and of practical interest. It
was again due to Louis Philippe, with the
assistance of new collaborators schooled by
experience. that the broken threads were re-
knotted with patience and with art. First
came the British alliance; second, the brilliant
return to traditional policies, to the Bourbonian policy of Spanish marriages; third, an

1. 1781-1855.

understanding with Metternich to try and avoid the troubles and revolutions fermenting in central Europe and which threatened France herself as much and in the same way as Austria.

It was sometimes objected to those who blamed the policy of the second Empire and the policy of nationalities : " How did you know that the course of history could have been changed ? By what means could the formation of German unity have been prevented ? "

It was, however, fairly simple and it would have been enough to continue the combinations of 1847. At this moment, Frederick William IV, abandoning the Holy Alliance, gave a glimpse of the shemes of Prussia by supporting the liberal German movement, by summoning the provincial Prussian States to proclaim before them his rupture with the so-called absolutism; in the end, by taking, against Austria and the smaller Courts, the direction of the unitarian and national movement in Germany. In this wise, the Prussian ambitions revived. Against these ambitions a tried alliance reformed itself ; that of France and Austria both having an equal interest in stopping the aggrandizement of Prussia and of protecting the independence of the secondary German States. The Entente was realized between Guizot and Metternich, such as it had been knotted, ninety years earlier, between Kaunitz and Bernis. It was, just as in 1756, a conservative alliance designed to present an overthrow of the old world, a displacement of the equilibrium of the forces of central Europe.

At this very time, indeed, a new agitation, stirred up by Palmerston[1], made its appearance in Italy. Guizot and Louis-Philippe were wisely opposed to the idea of Italian unity. It was no longer to be feared, as it had been a few years previously, that Austria would try to seize the whole Peninsula. There again Austria and France could come to terms. The agreement took place under the most auspicious and foresighted of conditions. Austria was suspected by Italy; so France was to be entrusted with the pacification of

1. British statesman (1784-1865).

Italy. France was feared in Germany : so Austria would take in hand the maintenance of order there. Excellent program, and of which one can all the better appreciate the merits in that it is in exact contrast to the course adopted by Napoleon III in 1859 and in 1866, and which led us to disaster in 1870:

" Hold fast, " was Metternich's watchword in February of 1848. At this moment France's situation in Europe was most favorable. Her position was the best vantage ground from which to await events. 1830 and 1840 were effaced. The Tsar himself abated his hostility to the Monarchy of July. As was written in the early days of 1848, France " had reconquered the right of dealing with world politics. "

At this very moment a new revolution broke out, a revolution which demanded as many " reforms " abroad as at home, and which was as much against exterior as against interior policies, which proclaimed the rights of " the people " even more than the rights of the French people, which was to be international, German, Italian, Polish, although it was to break out in Paris. It asserts its character, and its will, by beginning under the windows of the Ministry of Foreign Affairs to the cry of Poland and of Italy, in protest of Louis-Philippe's and Guizot's policies.

The revolution was ostensibly against the partisans of restricted suffrage, a suffrage not more enlightened, not more disinterested than universal suffrage, and surely less tractable and less obedient, as was just seen. The revolution was really made against what Carrel had called " the impertinent and cowardly system which proclaimed the political egotism of France. " The opposition, after having reproached Louis-Philippe with his efforts to maintain peace, accused him of betraying the cause of France in Europe, bound as it was to that of liberty and of nationalities. It was by the journalists, by the public speakers, that public opinion had been excited. From the parliamentary bench, where these reproaches had been but a pretext, they had passed to the crowd. They were concomitant with the insurrection

and the abuses which the parliamentary
middle classes made of this revolutionary
idealism bore, at this moment, their most
astounding fruits. Lamartine [1], when pleading the people's cause against Guizot, was at
least sincere. How could Thiers be so too?
Thiers, in his opposition against Guizot, had
made himself the supporter of the principle of
nationalities of which he was to be the adversary, ten years later, when the question was
to come up of opposing the Empire. In the
speech he pronounced on foreign affairs,
in February 1847, Thiers outlined, neither
more nor less, the principal scheme of the
policy of Napoleon III. The very faults which
Thiers himself denounced later to the "Corps
législatif," with an eloquence doubled by
righteousness, he suggested them, in a spirit
of opposition and rancor, to public opinion
and to the coming Government. This adversary of the Empire, just as much as any person
in France, paved the way for Louis Napoleon's
coup d'État.

1. Alphonse de Lamartine. French poet and statesman.
1790-1869.

The Monarchy of July fell at the very moment when the fermentation of Europe required, more than ever, on the part of France, a circumspect and far-seeing policy, Louis-Philippe, " because he was a Bourbon," had served the interests of the country. The Democracy had not understood him. And the parties had made game of him, exploiting his chimeras, his illusions, his generosity. 1848 was, if one likes to consider it so, the victory of the nation, but her victory against herself. France, henceforth, will be free to serve the cause of the people, to take up again, in Europe, the program of a revolutionary policy, free to sacrifice herself, to squander her chances, to compromise her security and her future. Some day the man will come who will execute the program before which the Second Republic recoiled. Once the last form of Monarchy banished, what will remain to defend with efficiency the French national interest ?

Lamartine, in the Chamber of the July Government, where he sat " on the ceiling[1]," exclaimed one day : " The resurrection of Italy would suffice to the glory of a nation." Suddenly brought to power by the revolution of February, the poet, with that intuitive intelligence of which he has several times given memorable evidence, understood that the Republic would ruin France, if she accomplished the policy of nationalities abroad. The day he took possession of the Ministry of Foreign Affairs, from which Guizot had just been ousted, one of the functionaries of the house, the highest in rank, the most experienced, who had been one of the artisans of the contract with Metternich, declared to the new Minister, after having transferred his duties to him, that nothing remained but to hand him his resignation " Not at all, " replied Lamartine, " you are our master and it is you whom I intend to consult. " Surprising homage rendered to Guizot and to Louis-Philippe. After having overthrown them, Lamartine was still to take his inspi-

---

1. When asked where he would take his seat, whether to right or left, or in the center, he answered (wishing to remain independent of partisanship) : " *On the ceiling.* "

ration from them, during his short tenure of office. Like them, he was to oppose " the policy the people were elaborating since 1815 " and which the victorious democracy thought it would see triumph with him. The poet, converted to good sense by his responsibility, was to disavow the revolutionary propagandists, their assaults in Savoy and beyond the Rhine, to implore the people to think first of France, before thinking of Germany, Italy, Ireland, Poland... During his long and melancholy retreat, did the poet ever dream that his brutal disgrace, his cruel unpopularity had come from this very adjuration ? Did he perceive that the lightning election of Louis Napoleon Bonaparte was to be foreseen when the prince, in his manifesto at Strassburg[1], had solemnly promised, as the heir of the Napoleonic name, and as the executor of the Saint-Helena will, to fight victoriously or die for the cause of the peoples.

Did Lamartine discern the meaning of the

1. In 1836, during Louis-Philippe's reign, Prince Louis Napoleon went to Strassburg, in an attempt to be crowned Emperor.

clamors which the mob shouted against him on that 15th of May, when his glory was extinguished? Did he know why, at the election of the 10th of December, the " man of Strassburg " had been elected, whilst he, the hero of February, obtained but a handful of votes? It may be.., but Lamartine never mentioned it. He never complained, no more than did Louis-Philippe or Charles X. He disdained to explain what he had wanted to do for his country. His secret is buried with him.

It was necessary for democracy to find in a second Napoleon the prevalence of its policy for the triumph of the cause of the people. The Second Republic had nurtured itself on its pure love of oppressed nationalities, and was glorified because of its determination to help them build their unity. Michelet has since related his feelings and his emotions, which were shared by all the other witnesses, when, on the celebration of the 4th of March 1848, in front of the church of the Madeleine, among the flags brought by the deputies of the exiled from the oppressed countries, was

" hoisted the great flag of Germany, so noble
(black, red and gold), the holy flag of
Luther, Kant and Fichte, Schiller, Beethoven
and beside it, the charming tricolor green
of Italy. " Recalling these memories which
were so dear to him, Michelet, twenty-two
years later, exclaimed : " What emotions!
How many vows for the unity of these
peoples, God grant us, we used to say,
to live to see a great and powerful Germany,
a great and powerful Italy. The European
council remains incomplete, inharmonious,
subject to the cruel whims, to the impious
wars of Kings, as long as these high perso-
nalities do not sit there in all their majesty,
and do not add a new element of wisdom
and of peace to the brotherly equilibrium
of the world. " A monument of all the
illusions of liberalism and of democracy ! A
text cruelly strange when read to-day, a text
which also throws light on our history and
which we will have to put as an epigraph to a
future philosophical history of the war of
1914.

However, the months which followed the

Revolution of February did not favor the cause of the people. The cause of Italian unity was defeated at Novare. German unity was wrecked in the Parliament of Francfort. This failure was also that of the German revolution, a copy of that of 1789, which aimed at founding a free German nation. For the revolution, and even the Republic, which so many of our contemporaries have fancied they saw in Germany's future, belong to her past.

The nationalists (as they would be called to day) promised to the German people the satisfactions and compensations they expected since 1815. They were, at the same time, liberals and, as Metternich called them, *Jacobins*. They thought they could realize German unity by a parliamentary and liberal regimen. The poets, the historians, the philosophers, the philologists who had spread, in opposition to the conservative and particularist forces of Germany, the idea of a revival of a German fatherland, also imagined they could be its builders. They were countless in the Francfort Parliament. Yet, their failure was rapid and complete. The Assembly had to separate after scenes of disorder and of massacre. The trial of a unification of Germany by liberalism was at an end. This was not the right way for German nationalism to succeed. Between liberalism and nationalism, the German patriots would have to choose. Soon, Bismarck was going to decide, and German unity, instead of engendering a great idealistic Republic, as Michelet and so many others supposed, was to resemble its creator, the Prussian State, monarchical, aristocratic, and war-like.

Whatever the political genius of Bismarck, everything shows, however, that he would not have succeeded in bringing forth German unity from the limboes to which the Francfort Parliament had banished it, if he had not found Napoleon III to assist him in his aims, and in the policy of nationalities.

Bismarck had a predecessor whose name is as obscure as his own is illustrious. This unlucky precursor had still the same plan : the unity of Germany by Prussian hegemony. Radowitz, in 1849, undertook, according to the same program as Bismarck, to make the Hohenzollerns the syndics of German patriotism, and to prove that they alone could succeed where the Francfort Parliament had failed. Still, Radowitz ended only in causing Prussia the humiliation of Olmütz, instead of leading her to Sadowa and Sedan. The reason was that he had found Austria and Russia, united to enforce the essential principles of the Treaties of 1815 and to bar the road to Prussia which would have brought her to the domination of Germany. Perhaps Prussia might have had even more than this to endure, bitter and mortifying as it was, and Austria might have seized this opportunity to retake Silesia. But Russia intervened in a moderating sense; it was the second time that Russia saved Prussia from ruin. She had already acted in the same way, under Frederick II. She was later to regret this movement of good-will and this erroneous calculation. All those who were helpful or indulgent towards the Prussian State have been brought, one after the other, to regret it.

The attempt of Radowitz, that luckless Bis-

marck, belongs to history none the less. It
is interesting because it proves, in contradiction to a wide-spread prejudice, that German
unity was neither inevitable nor necessary.
In order that it should prevail, it has been
necessary that France herself should have the
way, by overturning the barriers and by destroying the last guarantees of European order,
constituted by what remained of the principles
of the Treaty of Westphalia in the Treaties of
1815.

Here we touch again on one of the three or
four culminating points of our history. By
the enthusiastic election of Louis Napoleon, by
renewing to Napoleon III, Emperor, through
reiterated plebiscites the consecration of universal suffrage, French democracy has really
chosen her destiny. Under a Napoleon,
" the policy whith the people had been elaborating since 1815, " was at last to become a
fact. Napoleon III had received the mandate
to insure the triumph of the " cause of the
people " which he had sworn to uphold.
Never was an imperative mandate more conscientiously fulfilled. Never has French de-

mocracy had a more faithful servant of her wishes.

Some of the doctrinaire Republicans of 1848 had sulked Napoleon, after having advised the people to raise barricades against him. But their bitter reproach, that he had done away with liberty, softened, while the Emperor was realizing, in the democratic program, what the people really had most at heart, what represented the kernel of the doctrine. The attitude of Victor Hugo, in his voluntary exile, became ridiculous, when, from year to year, romanticism contemplated the realisation of the aims for the people's freedom to which the Empire was blindly attached. What Hugo had sung, Napoleon III achieved. The struggle against the powers of reaction and the gospel of the delivrance of Europe were again the subject of a celebrated poem in the *Châtiments*, just as they had inspired Beranger's[1] ditties, and hundreds of burning pages by Quinet and by Michelet. That struggle was started by the Second

1. Celebrated French song-writer (1780-1857).

Empire which took upon itself what the Second Republic had discarded. The system of Napoleon III was, moreover, that of a balance cleverly maintained. At home, it was by imposing the respect for order, religion and property that he satisfied the conservatives. Abroad, it was by his policy of nationalities that he fulfilled the wishes of the democrats : thus his position regarding universal suffrage was very strong. Later on, with the liberal Empire, he tried to change the terms of the equation. But the impulse was in full swing and what had been done could not be undone. By trying to turn back, the catastrophe was only hastened.

It has been said that Napoleon III's character was undecided. In his desire to conduct to success the policy of nationalities, he showed, however, until 1866, a determination from which nothing could divert him. In order to abolish the Treaties of 1815, which was the preliminary condition to a remodelling of Europe, Napoleon III proceded by skilfully-calculated stages. The first was the war against Russia. To weaken Russia, to lessen her prestige in Europe, was to end the Holy Alliance, and to render possible in the future a war against Austria aiming at the liberation of Italy. Democracy understood that calculation wonderfully, and foresaw that its desire was near fulfilment. The Crimean war, the war against Tsarism and autocracy, was a popular war. M. Gustave Geffroy has narrated, in *L'Enfermé*, how the revolutionist Barbès, in jail at the time (as he was usually), sent his congratulations, from his cell, to the man of the 2nd of December (Napoleon III), when he knew that the Empire was going to fight against Moscovite reactionarism.

Instructive concordance : Bismarck, in his " Souvenirs, " has related that his eyes began to open, that his deeply reactionary feelings of a Prussian country-squire changed, and that he ceased to be a partisan of the Holy Alliance from the time of the Crimean war, and that he, henceforth, conceived his plan to take advantage of each attempt of Napoleon III aiming at the destruction of the 1815 Treaties which had put Prussia in chains and made her powerless. Then, he would carry out his scheme for a united Germany and confer the reconstituted Empire upon the Hohenzollerns.

After Sebastopol and the Treaty of Paris, which gave him a leading position in Europe, Napoleon III could do anything, right as well as wrong. In full awareness he chose what was wrong. Vainly had Drouyn de Lhuys suggested a wise and prudent policy of European conservation, a return to the system of Guizot and Vergennes, an *entente* with Austria, which was becoming decreasingly dangerous. Napoleon III refused flatly. The peoples' cause constrained him to use his predominance in Europe first to liberate Italy. Russia, crippled, could no longer come to the rescue of Vienna. It was the war against Austria that Napoleon III deliberately willed, choosing to enfranchize Italy and create an Italian State.

The war of 1859 marks the zenith of the popularity of the Second Empire. Democracy, then, realized her power, admired and applauded herself as she saw her oldest aspirations satisfied by this war against Austria. Ancient traditions, passions inherited were

revived. The Attorney General Pinard, celebrated by Hugo's invectives, then made this
curious remark. " To find partisans for a
war in Italy, one has to hunt for them in the
centers where the fall of the Empire is plotted. " It was, under the crudest of forms,
the correct idea. The war against absolutist
and clerical Austria, the war for Italian liberation fired the liberals with enthusiasm, and
even such Republicans as had not slackened in
their resentment against the " Coup d'État. "
It was then that Jules Favre apostrophised
the Emperor in these terms : " If your will
is to destroy Austrian despotism, to deliver
Italy from its outrages, my heart, my blood,
my whole being is yours. " The day on
which Napoleon III took the train at the Gare
de Lyon to join our army in Lombardy, was
the apogée of his reign. Paris, in holiday
attire, smothered his carriage with flowers.
Even the Saint-Antoine quarter, where the
barricades of the 2nd of December had been
erected, cheered him heartily.

Magenta, Solferino, brilliant victories as
they were, had nevertheless caused French

blood to flow not for Italy alone. It was for Prussia, the enemy of to-morrow, that the Napoleonic democracy had toiled. Without hiding his satisfaction, Bismarck then said : " If Italy did not exist, we should invent her. " Already then, he perceived the possibility of ousting Austria from Germany, and of joining the young Italian State against her. Two more blunders on Napoleon III's part and Bismarck was to attain complete success.

These two blunders, the Napoleonic democracy, acting in conformity with its principles, did not fail to commit. It was, firstly, in the affair of the Duchies[1] where Bismarck insidiously involved Austria, in order to more certainly quarrel with her. In the name of the principle of nationalities, Bismarck claimed Schleswig-Holstein. In the name of the same principle of nationalities, Napoleon remained neutral and allowed Denmark to be crushed. Later, he felt it necessary to apologize and indeed with prodigious *naïveté*, as follows : " The Emperor, after having

1. Schleswig and Holstein taken from Denmark by Prussia, in 1864.

loudly proclaimed the principle of nationalities, could he, in regard of the banks of the Elbe, observe another line of conduct than the one he had adopted on the borders of the Adige? He was, however, far from supposing that the war, whose avowed aim was to free Germans from the Danish rule, would result in putting the Danes under German domination." Such is the danger of this famous principle, in which many, to-day, think they find the remedy for all the evils of Europe. The principle is double-edged : after having placed the Danes and the peoples of Alsace-Lorraine under Prussian tyranny, why whould it be incapable of creating other disorders producing other iniquities in the future?

The war of 1864 had afforded Bismarck the opportunity which he had sought for a rupture with Austria, in order to definitely expel this power from Germany. When the war of 1866 broke out, Napoleon III again found himself bound by his system to remain neutral. Moreover, was not Prussia the ally of Italy? To turn against Prussia, and take

the side of Austria, would have been a disavowal of the war of 1859, a reopening of the
whole question of Italian liberation. Even
had Napoleon III decided it, as Drouyn de
Lhuys, though unlistened to, had advised
him to do, public opinion would have put its
veto upon such a disavowal. Liberal and
Republican opinion and the whole of the
democratic press were aflame for the Prussian
cause, the cause of Italian unity and of German unity : a sincere and logical exaltation in
harmony with the traditions of democracy.
Bismarck boasted, later, of having fed this
enthusiasm by judiciously-distributed subsidies, and he has explained how, the day he
wanted war against France, it would be
enough for him to suspend these distributions
to weaken Prussophile sympathies. Gold
can play the role of a provocating agent, but
the world is led by ideas.

To understand the French policy of 1866,
the good understanding between Napoleon III
and public opinion, one must realize what
was the state of mind in France, four years
before Sedan. It is not from ignorance, cer-

tainly, that public opinion then sinned : it can be said that the nation chose her fate with open eyes. " The unity of Germany, like the unity of Italy, was the triumph of the Revolution, " remarked the *Siècle*. The *Liberté* demanded that France should remain faithful " to the policy of the predominance of a Protestant Prussia in Europe. " An idol of the people, Émile de Girardin[1], always peremptory, wrote in the *Presse* : " Let France keep calm, or draw the sword, France is logically on Prussia's side, because she is indissolubly bound to Italy. " And Peyrat, a Radical of still deeper dye, in his *Avenir National*, again insisted : " The war begun in Italy and in Germany, cannot fail to become general. The powers, neutral to-day, will be forced into it whether they like it or not, and France, notably, is called to play an eminent role. From the point of view of right, there is no more just cause than that of Italy ; from the point of view of our general interests and of our national honor, there is none more essentially

1. Celebrated french publicist. (1806-1881).

French. As far as Germany is concerned, the Emperor is not less explicit. His mind and design are clear. He recognizes that Prussia and the Germanic confederation naturally aim at giving to Prussia more homogeneity and strength to the North, and to the Confederation, a more solid union. It is Mr. de Bismarck's policy. Guéroult, in *l'Opinion nationale*, was not less favorable to the Imperial policy and the declaration of Napoleon III entirely satisfied his liberalism. " As for us, it would be the more difficult not to approve it as we are happy enough to meet there, robed in the lofty and substantial style of which the Emperor has the secret, the very views which we have not ceased to develop for nearly a year, concerning the causes of the German conflict, and, for seven years, concerning the solution of the crisis which is shaking Italy. " The *Journal des Débats* approved, in the name of doctrinaire liberalism : " The declaration contained in the Emperor's letter leaves no doubt as to the policy which the Government intends to follow in prevision of the events to come and, we must admit, this policy is congenial, in all its essential points, to our own ideas." Finally, the *Siècle*, still more explicit than its other *confrères*, declared : " Let it be well understood that to be with Prussia and Italy is to wish the triumph of the most just of all causes, and to remain loyal to the banner of democracy. And now, let the adversaries of Italy — and of Prussia — say frankly if they are for, or against, democracy and the Revolution."

Thus, to be with Prussia amounted, — even in 1866, — to be with democracy and with the Revolution ! How can we fail to evoke these reminiscences to-day ? What an overturning of the situations, what a use of the same formulæ, this time applied to Prussian militarism, and to Prussian reaction ! The historians of the future will perhaps jeer. But as for us, it is not by their irony that these variations of public opinion strike us. We are especially amazed by the errors of democracy, homicidal errors, which were to cost the lives of so many Frenchmen on the battlefields in the war of 1870, and of so many more on the battlefields in the war of 1914.

At the news of Sadowa, Paris, intoxicated with Republican doctrines, was illuminated. Indeed Paris of 1866 illuminated for the victory of Prussia. Was it not, as the *Siècle* said, a victory of the Revolution? And we were so few months from the terrible year of reckoning, the year of 1870. Never had a crowd cried more lustily: "Hurrah for my death... Death to my life!" When the truth became clear, when Thiers had issued his late vain warnings, when it was seen that Prussia was a formidable power, that she was to be the pivot of a new and mighty Germany, that, after Denmark and Austria, the turn of France would come, — then it was too late. Democracy was, more cruelly than ever, to pay for its blunders and its ignorance. And, in our turn, we are also making expiation for them. Never, and for no other people, has this Biblical text been more true : " The fathers have eaten a sour grape, and the children's teeth are set on edge. "

The policy which the people, poisoned

with utopistic international conceptions, had been elaborating since 1815 closed its cycle at Sedan. The ghosts of the Frenchmen whom the bullets of " liberal Prussia, " of the " natural ally " of France, then killed, could repeat, with those killed to-day, the great apostrophy of the wisest poets in antiquity : " Delicta Majorum. " It is through the faults of our fathers that we perish. Our fate, our tomb, was prepared by those before us.

CHAPTER VI

History, when considered like a panorama, shows how unyielding is the logic with which events are linked together and engendered. But this mechanism is slow. The links are scattered over a long series of years and they present a fearful complexity to the eyes of statesmen who catch their meaning and know that a germ, good or bad, sown in the political soil may perhaps bear fruit only long after they have themselves disappeared. Such examples abound in the epochs of our history of which we have just taken a birdseye view.

The benefit which Louis-Philippe[1] bestowed on our country by the creation of the neutrality of Belgium has only now begun to bear its full effect. In the same manner, the errors of the Revolution and of the Empire have only shown all their fatal consequences in the light of time. It is in the same way that the war of 1870, together with the direct effects of defeat on our country, has had for the whole of Europe, indirect effects which slowly formed the situation out of which the great war was to come.

After 1870, when German unity was a fact, and the German Empire founded, the supreme guarantees of Europe against the abuse of force disappeared together with the last traces of the Treaties of Vienna and of Westphalia. " There is no longer a Europe, " is the word which cardinal Antonelli[2] first enunciated and which has been repeated a hundred times. Since the unity of Germany, there

1. Louis-Philippe I, 1830-1848. Born in 1773. Son of the Duke of Orléans, who, at the time of the Revolution, took the name of Philippe-Egalité. Died at Claremont (England) 1850.

2. Prime Minister of Pope Pius IX (1866-1876).

are no vestiges of that ancient system of Europe which had organized itself for better or for worse against the possible excesses of the strongest. The system of equilibrium which the European world had established, thanks to France, and which was based essentially on the impotence of Germany, has been destroyed. Once Germanism at liberty, the reign of force reappeared in the ancient commonwealths still more aggravated by the powerful concentration of modern States and by the resources of Science : terrible retrogression in an age when men had never been so certain of their progress.

After Prussia had destroyed the last conventions of the Society of Peoples, the other States, it must be granted, freed themselves in their turn, and in the same manner. 1870 marks the advent of international anarchy. Though egotism normally rules the life of nations, there are circumstances when absolute egotism costs dear. In the disorder into which the decline of ancient principles, the antagonism of nationalities, and the blunders of the Napoleonic democracy had thrown

Europe, each government witnessed the defeat of our country with the thought of using the opportunity presented. Thiers felt this bitterly when he undertook, through the capitals of Europe, that painful journey whose object was to gain support for our country. It is related, that, having arrived in London, and whilst he was advocating the cause of France in Lord Granville's [1] study, the old man, worn out by fatigue, suddenly collapsed, speechless. Lord Granville thought him dead, and was greatly impressed by the dramatic beauty of the end of this illustrious statesman, succumbing at the very moment when he was pleading for his vanquished country.

It was not only with this esthetic indifference that England, in 1870, looked on our reverses. Thoroughly unconscious of the German peril which was then, for her, only in its cradle, England conducted herself in such a way that no one could come to our aid. She organized the League of Neutrals which could only do harm to France by

1. British Statesman (1815-1891).

prohibiting its members from taking part in the war separately; it was exactly the opposite of the Convention of London, signed in September 1914. Gladstone[1] and the liberal party, who governed Great Britain then, shouldered a heavy responsibility towards their country. By letting the German Empire force its way on to the world stage, these pacifists prepared for the future a war which their successors have been obliged to face. For it is again by one of these reversions of earthly things which are familiar to the student of History, that England was forced to declare war on Germany in 1914, and another generation of liberals could not avoid the throwing down of the gauntlet.

England, at this time, was not the only one amongst the powers to take her full liberty. Never were so many treaties torn up, never so many signatures disowned as in 1870. When Vittorio Emanuele[2] entered Rome, he repu-

1. Leader of the Liberals (1809-1893).
2. Vittorio Emanuele, King of Sardinia, 1849 and later, of Italy, 1860. The founder, with his Minister Cavour, of Italian unity (1820-1878).

diated the Convention of September. Russia, overlooking the results of the Crimean war, provoked a revision of the Treaty of Paris. Each one freed himself from obligations and contracts. Many Bismarckian aphorisms upon right and force have been quoted. But, who was the Minister who then stated that written right founded on treaties no longer had the same moral sanction that it might have had in earlier times? It was Gortschakof, the Chancellor of the Russian Empire.

The Duc de Broglie[1] has related that, when he was delegated by Jules Favre[2] to the London Conference, he set out with one hope and one ambition : to begin again the work of Talleyrand at Vienna, to return to France by diplomacy what she had lost by war. He quickly awoke to the reality that the international conference excluded from its debates

1. Minister of Marshall Mac-Mahon, second President of the French Republic (1821-1901).

2. Celebrated lawyer and political man. Proposed the downfall of the Empire, in 1870, after the capitulation of Sedan. Then became a member of the Government of the national defence (1809-1880).

those questions concerning France and Germany. Times had changed since 1815, also circumstances. And the Duc de Broglie, till then much more of a liberal than a royalist, regretted that he was not supported, as Talleyrand had been, by another Louis XVIII.

Vanquished and bruised, France of 1871 for one moment thought of the Monarchy as an ancient and tried instrument of national recovery. The disappointment was immense and the French people had just been awakened out of their dream by a terrible shock. Invasion, two provinces gone, more than a million Frenchmen snatched from their country, an autocratic and military monarchy laying its hands on all Germany, and Germany accepting the Prussian hegemony : such was, indeed, the catastrophe which proceeded from the principles of Revolution, the " cause of the people " and the spreading of liberal ideas. Then, the French people, acknowledging their illusions, renounced all great exterior action, shut themselves up, and became absorbed by their interior reorganization.   A new era, a new experience was to begin for them.

In the course of the years which immediately followed the Treaty of Francfort, it can be said that democracy had really made its conscience examination.   It is true that she did not conclude by recognizing her errors, neither did events absolve her.   Forgetting the imperative mandate she had foolishly given to Napoleon III, repeated approbations she had showered on his policy, she heaped all the responsibility for the disaster on " personal power. "   The Monarchists themselves, at the " Assemblée Nationale, " shared in great part the conviction that so-called " personal power " had been the cause of our calamities.   It is the sentiment expressed by the Duc d'Audiffret-Pasquier [1], when he said : " We will bring back the King, but tied like a sausage. "   The result was that there was no King at all, either

1. French political man.   Member of the French Academy. President of the Senate in Marshall Mac-Mahon's time 1823-1905).

" tied " or otherwise. It is essentially on that idea that the restoration of the Monarchy was stranded. The Republican parliamentary regime, the integral democracy, henceforth, had won the game and Bismarck, he professed it frankly, welcomed this solution with a smile. Much more, he boasted, at several critical dates of our interior conflicts, to have " stage-managed from Berlin. " The Monarchy of the Hohenzollerns did for France what the Capetians had formerly done for Germany : it saw with satisfaction in our midst the very institutions which were contrary to hers. And, referring to the attitude to be observed towards the affairs of France, Bismarck gave to his master the same advice as Pierre Dubois had given to Philippe le Bel, and Marillac to Henri II, concerning German affairs.

While France was debating the question of whether she would be a Monarchy or a Republic, the planet continued to turn and European problems to puzzle. Even with Italian

unity and German unity accomplished, quiet
was not yet established in Europe. The
Oriental question, continuously developing,
and more continuously entangled in European
affairs since the xviii[th] century, was extending, and under acuter forms. As Proudhon[1] had foreseen, new nationalities aspired
to secure their place in the sun, claimed their
right to independence and to life. Some
peoples, formerly overlooked, such as the
Asiatic tribes (it must be remembered what
the Bulgarians were for Voltaire), began to
realize their existence. The conception of
races began to reach the confines of the European world. The Slavonic idea was attaining
the virulence of a ferment similar to the
Germanic idea in the preceding period. It
was to be the origin of new and vast struggles
which anarchy and European rivalries would
envenom.

The Russo-Turkish war, the great national
war of Russia, the war of the deliverance of
the oppressed Slav brothers, had ended with

1. French publicist, author of a famous Socialist theory
(1809-1865).

the Congress of Berlin[1], the scene of Bismarck's most subtle intrigues. France, though represented at this Congress of Europe, was however morally absent. Public opinion, to which these Oriental affairs were as new as they were distant, threw but inattentive glances on them. Very natural inattention. Yonder, nevertheless, the storms of the future were brewing and the War of 1914 emerged from the Berlin Congress, as the plant emerges from the seed. Bismarck had reckoned on the uneasiness which the progress of Russia would inspire to England, in order to slip between the two powers and make use of their rivalry. On the other hand, he had seized the opportunity to seduce Austria, to fasten her definitely to Germany by showing her the road to the East as a compensation for Sadowa. The chief aim of his plan was the attribution of Bosnia and Herzegovina to the Austro-Hungarian Empire, Where is the Frenchman who then guessed that, on his account, his country would,

1. 1878.

thirty-five years later, be drawn into war? The British did not imagine it either. Still more, England herself entered into Bismarck's combination. It was Lord Salisbury who, by a well prepared scenario, suggested that the administration of the two provinces should be entrusted to Austria. Thus Austria found herself placed in an antagonism, to be fought out sooner or later, but ineluctably, with the Serbs, with Russia and the Slav commonwealth. To-day, England is the ally of the Russians. She is at war against Austria and Germany. And one of the immediate causes of this war was the definite annexation of Bosnia and Herzegovina by the Emperor Francis Joseph. Who can foresee the changes in the points of view, in interests, in situations that the future may again recall?

Long years of armed peace prevailed while this conflagration was smouldering. Then, one saw the French nation drop little by little the idea of revenge and not without feeling, at intervals, the spur of a German

threat, indulge in the illusion of all democracies, which consists in giving to interior
political questions the first place. All democracies are inclined to live as in a sealed
alambic. That peasant whose horizon is
circumscribed by his field, that proletarian
whose only fortune is his two arms, that
merchant weighed down by worry, and
even, in higher spheres, that physician, that
lawyer, whom their profession specializes,
how could they turn attention with adequate continuity beyond the frontiers? In
the French Chamber, mirror of the middle
classes, exterior political questions have never
been discussed save by a small number of
parliamentarians, always the same, listened to
with the deference granted by those supposed
to possess the key to all the mysteries, but
listened to without attention. In fact, all the
Ministers of Foreign Affairs during the Government of the Republic were allowed to
follow the policy they liked : the Parliament
gave them a blank cheque. The French
democracy, above all, set about a redistribu-
tion of wealth. Her main preoccupation has

been taxes, salaries, pensions, and her policy was, firstly, fiscal. Her care has been to divide the capital of the nation, not to increase it, nor even to protect it. At the same time, one saw in England a similar tendency leading the electoral body and the Parliament. According to the often repeated sentence of Lord Rosebery in his campaigns against British radicalism and which will perhaps serve later to characterize the attitude of France and of England during the years which preceded the war, the chief occupation of these two countries was to create a kind of chimerical Eden without caring to know if wolves would not be tempted to storm the fold.

However the monstrous State erected by Prussia in Germany weighed on the life of the whole of Europe. That vast autocratic and military monarchy was not only dangerous by its organisation and its power, the very conditions of its formation obliged it to grow incessantly to arm itself more and more every day. As if they had felt that the existence of United Germany was an abnormal phenomenon, the founders of the new Empire thought (and so did their successors) that this Empire could only last by being sustained by an immense military strength, by keeping always at hand the means of intimidating and attacking, at its own time, those neighbours whose possible coalition was Bismarck's nightmare. Thence came the theory of a " preventive war ".

There was yet something more. The prestige of Germany was based on her victories. She had built up her credit throughout the world, from the political point of view, from the commercial point of view, and even from the point of view of her " Cultur, " on her military superiority. Nietzsche said one day that, in the way of poets, artists, philosophers, new Germany had Bismarck, and again Bismarck, and only Bismarck. Contemporary Germany has, indeed, lived on the authority bestowed on her by the three successive victories of Prussia, these three wars of 1864, of 1866 and 1870 of which Sir Edward Grey said so eloquently that they had been three wars declared against Europe. The system which, first, Prussia, and second, the German Empire, had founded, could but become worse. Things are maintained in the same conditions which have presided at their birth : United Germany has continued to flourish by the same means which had drawn her out of the dust, that is to say, by war, considered as a national industry. This is the idea that her Chancellors, though so different, have never failed to develop. Always more soldiers, always more cannons, Germany had to possess regiments like a State Bank must possess gold in its safes to give value to its banknotes : M. de Bethmann-Hollweg again exposed this theory, and but a short time before the war. An hour came when the temptation to use this metal reserve was too strong. The great delusion of Europe has been to believe that the German Empire could keep nine hundred thousand men of the first line under arms simply to preserve peace, that this military power, one of the most formidable the world has ever seen, would not exalt the people who disposed of it, would not impel to plans of conquest and aggression.

The great nations which by indifference, blindness or reckoning, had let Prussia take hold of the German Empire, had, however, not gone far before feeling the edge of the peril. In 1871, Charles Gavard, one of our best diplomats, in London at that time, noted the following in his diary : " The British public understands that it is the perpetual war which now begins. " A fleeting intuition, of course. Bismarck did his best to dissipate it by exciting England against Russia. But as early as 1875, whilst he was planning once for all to finish off France, the triple Entente spontaneously delineated itself as a natural necessity. Some time had yet to elapse before it shaped itself. Still, it can be stated that the opposition of the three powers allied to-day, and their conflict with the German Empire were inscribed on the scroll of fatality from the very day when Germany as a block appeared on the stage.

It is to the great honor of the French nation that through all her wanderings and weaknesses, she has kept intact the idea of her independence and the consciousness of her duties. We have, in the course of this book, shown the errors and responsibilities of democratic governments. But what must be loudly proclaimed is that never perhaps in history will there have been seen a people ruled by democracy able to put forth such a rigor-ous resistance as ours to the principles of dis-solution which its institutions involved. A democracy which, during forty-four years, has fully accepted the heavy burden of obliga-tory and universal service, is one of the rarest phenomena in the annals of mankind. France, and how bitterly we have cause to feel it, should have armed and prepared herself even more thoroughly to withstand the last German aggression. Her great title to glory will be that she assumed the necessary sacrifices. In 1914, she took up the German gauntlet. She is now making an effort, she is showing a perseverance that history will admire, an energy which does honor to the resources of the race. We may say with truth : no other country but France would have been capable of that strain. What would not have been our destiny if, at home, foresight had equalled courage, if the brain of the State had been as good as the heart of its citizens ?

A few years ago, — if we can be forgiven for quoting ourselves, — we wrote that it had never been more seasonable to recall the famous metaphor of Prevost-Paradol[1] before 1870. Those two engines colliding on the same track and of which Prevost-Paradol had spoken towards the end of the Second Empire, represented no longer only France and Prussia : they were the Germanic World, on one side, the Triple Entente, on the other. A commonplace, generally adopted, developed in numberless speeches and newspapers, has been to maintain as far as the day of the declaration of war that the Triplice and the Triple Entente had reconstituted the equilibrium of Europe, that the two systems of Alliances balanced one another and that the risk of war was thereby discounted. A very dangerously

1. French publicist. Was appointed, under the Empire, French Minister at Washington, where he died (1829-1870).

unstable equilibrium indeed. France, Russia, England, in spite of all that could have separated them, had ended by joining against the common peril. But, had this coalition existed only on paper, it was enough to make Germany fear her end and especially to appear no more longer in the guise of the strongest. It was necessary that the belief in her military superiority should remain intact. Hence, always increasing armaments and a greater strain each time a new event arose on the political horizon, and seemed likely to lessen German prestige in Europe. On its side, the Triple Entente, mostly with regret and always with reluctance and delay, was bound to keep even with the German Empire. This parallel move of the two groups could not continue indefinitely. Such rivalry could only end in war.

The Triple Entente only followed the impulsions coming from Berlin. She simply replied, and nearly always insufficiently, to the measures taken by Germany. She remained faithful, in a word, to the principles, which had presided over her origin : the principle of resistance, the principle of non-acceptance, in answer to the express will of Germany to dominate always by the might of her arms, to impose her decrees by intimidating Europe. The provocation could not spring from the Anglo-Franco-Russian group. But the obstacles that this group opposed to German supremacy, the growing efforts to which it obliged the Empire, embittered the latter more and more each day. Ten times Germany attempted to break up the Triple Entente. In spite of its hesitations, its deficiencies, its failures, the Triple Entente has lasted. The more Germany was arming, multiplying threats and provocations, the firmer was the Triple Entente. The day was to come when Germany would try to break it; thus, what was done to preserve peace would become a germ of conflict. Such was again one of the fatalities paving the way to the European war.

A state in which all is born of the war idea leads to war, but also a state in which war is the " national industry, " does not, however, run any great risk, unless some peculiar set of circumstances arises. Germany, while decided on a preventive war against Russia, on an aggressive war against France, missed perhaps better opportunities than the one she chose in 1914. After twenty years of a peaceful reign, it was in 1909, concerning Oriental affairs, that for the first time, William II adopted a clearly warlike attitude, and why ?

The Turkish revolution of 1908, the definite annexation of Bosnia-Herzegovina by Austria, the protestation of Russia, and a general resistance of Slavism against the rush of the Germanic world towards the East, the linking of these causes is evident. But we must go back further, we must understand that Germany, at the congress of Berlin, while attributing Bosnia to Austria, to buy her alliance, while granting her a compensation for her defeat of 1866, bound herself for the future. This compensation had to be guaranteed to Austria, under the penalty of seeing the latter aim at a resumption of her role in the Germanic commonwealth from which she had been expelled after Sadowa. In the meantime, the Balkan peoples had definitly become conscious of their existence. As a few penetrating spirits had foreseen, after Proudhon, the principle of nationalities, diffused in Oriental Europe, was producing there the same upheaval that it had caused in Central Europe. Russia was at the back of Serbia as Napoleon III had been at the back of Piedmont. Conflicts of ideas, of feelings, of interests, everything contributed to the world conflagration. Russia found it possible to yield to the German ultimatum of 1909 enjoining her to recognize the annexation of Bosnia-Herzegovinia by Austria. But even had she yielded again to the ultimatum of 1914, had Germany registered a new success of her policy of intimidation by obtaining from Russia the permission for Austria to crush the Serbs, an analogous situation would sooner or later have presented itself. A day was to come when a deep opposition, dictated by the instinct of conservation, would check Germany's further strides, lest the Germanic world should put its yoke on Europe.

Germany has failed in her enterprise. The Triple Entente, as M. Viviani[1] declared, did not give way to the pressure exerted on it. It has suffered the trial of war and withstood it. France has remained faithful to her alliance with Russia, although William II, as indicated by the preliminary warnings of Herr von Schoen[2] at Paris, had discounted a lessening of fidelity. Belgium, by a national feat which will remain for ever graved in history, rejected the summons of the mighty Empire. England, unexpectedly for the Emperor and his people, was careful not to renew her blunder of 1870. In spite of the power of her armies, the most formidable war machine that the world has ever seen, in spite of her generations of preparation and an organization carried to a perfection never yet attained, Germany was beaten on the banke of the Marne, and since then her military supremacy has been a matter for discussion. Neutrals no longer put their faith in her invincibility, — weighty change in the European atmo-

1. Head of the French Cabinet, in August 1914.
2. German Ambassador at Paris. July 1914.

sphere. Above all Europe has learnt that her tranquillity, her security, her civilization are incompatible with the existence of a great and united Germany, and that no understanding is possible with her. Whatever happens, one truth will remain in the minds of all : that German might is the scourge of the European commonwealth.

However bright the future may appear, let us not forget that history favors complexity and that it abhors simple solutions. So many interests, aspirations, needs, forces are facing each other that it is wiser to doubt, even after this gigantic conflict, that a new and final order, satisfactory to all, can be brought about by a stroke of the wand. It is important to remember that policies live mostly on compromises, on average solutions, which leave an open door to new difficulties and to new struggles. The idea of nationality, the idea of race has been travailing Europe since a hundred years. Who can say that these ideas will not spur on, in their turn, other peoples who to-day are slumbering, that they will not stir up other catastrophies?

France was directly affected by German unity. She has just, by a counterstroke, endured a tremendous war arising from the consequences of this unity, and brought on by the birth and needs of new nations in Oriental Europe. Who can assure us that these causes shall cease to work, or that similar events will not give a similar blow to our destinies?

The hope we can cherish is that if Germany is thoroughly beaten, the regime she has imposed on the world and which, by a dreadful retrogression, has placed under arms the whole male population of Europe (a thing which would have horrified the French in former times), can and must be abolished. War after the German fashion, the savage war of armed nations, will then become the saddest record of mankind. The century during which Germany was united and mighty will be counted as the Iron Century. As to knowing complete tranquillity, as to the assurance of being able to live for themselves, on themselves, and safe from new conflicts, it will be long before the nations may enjoy any such heavenly comfort of mind.

History is slow, its reversions, its meanderings, are perfidious.   One of the worst delusions a nation can breed consists in believing that, by her will alone, she can escape the consequences of the past, that she can with safety declare that, for her, all problems are solved and, that, satisfied with what is within her boundaries, she will live for herself alone.

This delusion which has tempted almost all democracies, has nearly cost us our national existence.   It is the error into which France must not fall again.   The French of 1914 have heroically paid for the blunders of their ancestors.   They have prepared for the generations to come a better future than the age they have known themselves.   But, even for these coming generations, the cycle of toil and trouble is not, and never will be, terminated.

THE END

NOTICE CONCERNING THE MAPS

*These maps and their summaries have been prepared
and brought out by Mr. Robert Doré, former pupil of the
School of Charts, of Paris, patented archivist-paleograph.*

FRANCE AND THE ROYAL STATE

AT THE ACCESSION OF HUGUES CAPET IN 987

1. — This map shows, firstly, the boundaries of
Gaul under the Roman rule. These limits suffered
no change as long as the Roman Empire lasted, that
is to say during the four first centuries of the Christian
era. Gaul, as is shown, was comprised between the
Rhine, the Alps, the Pyrenean Chain and the Atlantic
Ocean. During the Carolingian times, the country
properly called France was, as a whole, the land
situated between the Seine and Rhine. During the
xth century, the word " France " shall have the same
meaning as " Gaul. "

Secondly, the map points out the limits of France
at the time of Hughes Capet's accession to the throne,
in 987. These limits present no difference with those
fixed by the Treaty of Verdun in 843. This famous

treaty removed, from the French dominion, the immense territory ranging from the North Sea to the Mediterranean and which henceforth composed the Duchy of Lorraine, in the North, and the Kingdom of Burgundy, in the South. We must observe that the said territory had, during eight centuries, belonged, first, to Roman Gaul, then to the Kingdom of the Franks, finally to the Empire of Charlemagne, whose capital was at Aix-la-Chapelle. It is this very country which was the center of the Carolingian policy, policy entirely inspired by Roman tradition and whose chief aim was to check the Germans in the North, and the Arabs, in the South.

Thirdly, the same map shows, around Paris, the narrow estate directly owned by Hughes Capet who possessed only a right of paramount lordship over the rest of France. Therefore, the royal policy shall aim, firstly, inland, at grouping, around the crown, all the fiefs composing the Kingdom ; secondly, outside the country, at recovering the estates which, historically, belonged to France, Gaul's natural heir. During eight hundred years, the Capetians will fulfill their task : the Revolution destroyed the work when it was near its achievement.

GERMANY IN THE MIDDLE AGES

2. — After the Treaty of Verdun, the German portion of the Carolingian Empire, that is to say the land enclosed between the Rhine, the Alps, the river Elbe and the Sea, was divided into four great Duchies : Saxony, Franconia, Germania, Bavaria.   When, after a period of confusion, Duke Henry of Saxony assembled these States under his rule and founded the Kingdom of Germany (919), the Kingdom of Lorraine could not maintain its independence and was incorporated first, to Germany, then to the Empire, when the Imperial dominion was restored by Othon 1, in 962. This very country shall remain henceforth, between France and Germany, the stake of a thousand years, struggle.

The white part of the map shows the Kingdom of Germany in 919 and, the " Marches, " or defensive territorial organizations, which Othon I established beyond the Danube and the Elbe in order to contain and repel the Slavs and the Hungarians.   The boundaries traced on the map, remained unchanged from the end of the xv^{th} century, until the Holy Empire's suppression in 1805, save at the Weser where they suffered, in favor of France, the modifications shown by map n° 3.   We must observe that Prussia, a Slav country conquered by the Teutonic knights, will still remain outside the Empire.

The growth within these limits is quite different from what occurs in France. While France becomes unified by degrees, while her former feudal divisions are changed into administrative districts, Germany crumbles. At the Emperor Frederic II's death (1250), the separatist tendencies, till then restrained, get their free play to such an extent, that the four hundred German states, chaotically aggregated under the Imperial sceptre, remain almost harmless for France whose boundaries, although open on that side, remain inviolate.

This parcelling can only be shown on the map approximately.

FRANCE

FROM 987 TO 1797

3. — This map shows, firstly, what were the increases to French territory from 987 to the Treaties of Westphalia, in 1648 ; then, the further progress realized in 1658, through the Treaty of the Pyrenees, direct consequence of the Westphalian Treaties.

At that time Germany, thanks to the reduction of her territory in general, and to the parcelling of her constitutive elements, had reached the utmost degree of military impotence. One must bear in mind that Metz and Alsace, incorporated to the Kingdom in 1552 and 1648 respectively, remained segregated from the French soil through the Duchy of Lorraine which will only be embodied in 1766. Strassburg remains a free city until 1681.

Furthermore, the map shows the territorial progress realized by France from 1659 to January 1st, 1792. These limits were those left to France by the first Treaty of Paris (May 30th 1814). Finally the map shows the territories taken from France through, the second Treaty of Paris, after Waterloo (November 20th, 1815).

The six cities lost by France at her North-Eastern boundary are underlined; that loss seriously endangered the safety of that side of the country. Such was for France the territorial ransom she had to pay for the last Napoleonic attempt.

GERMANY
FROM 1648 TO 1914

4. — Germany, who, during the Middle Ages, had led a thorny life through the most disorderly political system, had started a constructive evolution at the hands of the Hohenzollerns. At first, Margraves of Brandenburg, then Electors, finally, in 1702, Kings of Prussia, they will revive, against the Habsburgs and against France, the idea of a Germanic Empire.

The map shows : 1° the possessions of the Elector of Brandeburg in 1648 ; 2° the increases obtained by the Prussian Monarchy from 1648 to 1815. We must observe that, in 1789, Prussia possessed, in the valley of the Rhine, but small estates, separated from each other, among principalities of a lay or ecclesiastic character. The mediatisations, on one hand, and the secularisations, on the other, operated between 1803 and 1810, have made a whole conglomerate of these territories which formed thenceforth the two provinces of Westphalia and of Rhenan Prussia.

As shown by the map, these two provinces remained still segregated, in 1815, from the rest of the Prussian Kingdom, through the Kingdom of Hanover, the Electorate of Hesse and the Dukedom of Brunswick.

The concentration of the German territories into the hands of rulers less numerous than in the past, was a result of French influence. But this influence, of

Revolutionary stamp, was bound to bear the worst fruits.

The map shows furthermore : 3° the States annexated or submitted by Prussia from 1815 till 1870, and the limits of the Confederation of Northern Germany at the head of which was the King of Prussia at the eve of the Franco-German war ; 4° the States of Southern Germany which were joined to those of the North, on the 18th of January 1871, in order to build the present German Empire ; also, the countries robbed of France, that is to say, Alsace with part of Lorraine.

Paris. — Typ. Philippe Renouard, 19, rue des Saints-Pères. — 54569.

I. — FRANCE AND THE ROYAL ESTATE AT THE ACCESSION OF HUGHES CAPET IN 987.
II. — GERMANY IN THE MIDDLE AGES.
III. — FRANCE FROM 987 TO 1797.
IV. — GERMANY FROM 1648 TO 1914.
NOUVELLE LIBRAIRIE NATIONALE